Praise for *Behold, I Make All Things New!*

"This book is a compendium for all people in difficult situations and are asking the question of where is God? or why has the good God allowed this to happen to me? It is an antidote for depression caused by troubles of life. Its academic, theological, spiritual, and practical richness makes it useful for readers from different backgrounds. It is a must-read for all who want to finish their life's journeys well."

> — Reverend (Dr.) Samson Olasupo A. Ayokunle, President, Christian Association of Nigeria & Co-Chairman, Nigeria Inter-Religious Council (NIREC)

"Put on your thinking cap as you read this book. Do not try to skim through its pages…When you have completed a thorough and considered reading of this book; you will be better equipped to minister the gospel to the unbelieving – whether they be atheist, agnostic or simply the unconcerned or uncaring. You will also be able to encourage and strengthen the believer in his or her resolve to live out the Christ-life with boldness as they minister to and encourage those around them."

> — Reverend W. Doyle Bell, Tallahassee, Florida, USA

"Since time immemorial, whenever bad/evil things happen, people can't help but wonder why it has happened and where God is in all of these. In this book, the author has made a commendable effort to provide answers to these questions. This book is recommended for all Christians to help them through seemingly difficult times and equip them to minister to unbelievers."

> — Reverend (Dr.) Mathew O. Olaniyan, Fmr. President, Oyo Baptist Conference, Oyo State, Nigeria

"Whether you come to this text as a Jesus-follower or an atheist, you will be offered help and hope from a logical and thoroughly biblical answer as to why a good, all-powerful God allows such evil to happen in this world. Do we want God to zap away all evil now? That would include all humanity. Do we want only the evil we experience to be done away with? That would be untenable. Wherever you land in this discussion of theodicy, Babatunde Agboola offers a conclusion with the best, no, the only option that provides real answers, real hope in this evil world. There is a purpose beyond the pain when one understands the goodness and wisdom of God over humanity. This scripture-driven text shows us that the Christian God is not caught off guard by the evil in His good creation. He sees, He cares, and He knows the end of evil is on the way. Be comforted that God is at work, especially when you are devastated by your painful trials. "

— Pastor Butch Smith, Texas, USA

"In almost 25 years of practicing journalism during which I have read many books, including authoring a few and editing several others, never have I come across a book that affected my Christian faith like *Behold, I Make All Thing New!* To say the book is inspiring is understating the fact. It is more than an inspiration. It is actually a revelation of how God wants us to deal with pain and unpalatable events in life…The author, who I have known for close to 30 years, presents his personal experience of pain in a gripping manner that exposes biblical and intellectual concepts, helping to resolve many knotty issues surrounding life's challenges in a way that encourages us to trust in the all-knowing God to have the final say."

— Sunday Oguntola, Online Editor, The Nation Newspaper, Lagos, Nigeria

"…The book *Behold, I Make All Things New!* was borne out of the furnace of his personal experience of pain and suffering in raising a beautiful daughter but with a genetic disorder, combined with his deep quest to provide an intelligent and rational response to the dilemma of reconciling the existence of evil and suffering with an omnipotent, omnibenevolent, and omniscient God. The book is a masterpiece, a comprehensive apologia of the faith and the hope that believers have in God—undergirded by sound scriptural reflections, and an encouragement for those going through pain, suffering, and different challenges of life…a MUST read for everyone…"

> — Reverend Damilola Abraham, Lead Pastor, The Love Community Church, London, United Kingdom

Behold, I Make All Things New! is probably the best book you will love to read. The author has done an excellent job of exonerating and establishing the existence of God biblically in the presence of evil as he addresses this crucial issue of theodicy in this work."

> — Dr. Jacob K. Oladipupo, Pastor, Great-Commission Christian Church, San Antonio Texas, USA

"This book is a MUST read for everyone seeking answers to very difficult questions of life, particularly concerning the existence of evil, in the presence of a good God. The book brings scientific perspectives and logical reasoning to prove the authenticity of the all-powerful, all-knowing, omnipresent, and good God. I commend Caleb's intellectual prowess and diligence in bringing out from the word of God what to some people may look like contradictions and quietly proved the scriptural passages not to be contradictions with many facts from the Bible and many other extant scientific literature. Highly recommended for both believers and unbelievers! God bless you."

> — Dr. Adeoye Adegorite, Management Consultant, Provincial Government of Ontario, Canada.

3

"For a long time, I have been searching for a material like this book that my brother was graciously given to write, that would shed more light on how God who Himself is Love allows evil to happen, despite His ability and power to prevent them. In my search I stumbled upon a book titled "the splendor of His Ways " by Stephen Kaung a contemporary of Watchman Nee, and now together with this new book *Behold, I Make All Things New!*" I'm firmly rooted on the subject matter. No one after going through this book cannot but exult in praise and adoration to God for His infinite wisdom that is beyond human comprehension. I pray that the Lord will give this book wings and use it as a blessing to our generation. I greatly recommend this book."

— Tommy Akanni, Houston, Texas, USA

"When a thoroughly trained and practicing engineer writes about faith from a personal experience built on a solid biblical foundation, readers are certainly in for a treat! Not a lot of books exist that offer a balanced engagement with the problems of evil and human suffering using both the spiritual and rational lenses. I am thrilled at this amazing piece of work, evidence that good theology has room for both perspectives, with everything leading ultimately to a vision of the goodness of a God that is good by nature. I recommend this masterpiece to anyone struggling to make sense of unpalatable experiences in personal, national, or even global spheres. It offers rich benefits to people of all types and levels of belief. This work is a powerful contribution that can lead to human flourishing here on earth while hoping joyfully for the coming perfection when God makes all things new!"

— Oloyede Odeyale, IT Engineer, Lagos, Nigeria.

"This is a feast for the soul and spirit. The author of *Behold, I Make All Things New!*" takes on one of the most difficult questions facing our troubled age as we cry out "where is God amidst the ravages of war, the abduction of innocent children by terrorists, the heartbreak of seeing loved ones endure sickness, and the unremitting grief of death and loss?" Caleb Agboola responds in this tender ode of a father pondering the desperate pain of the path his family has journeyed with their precious daughter Ayanfe, who was born with a genetic condition. But he also brings the powerful inquiry of a thirsty believer, the riveting insight of a prophet, and the provocative rigor of a theologian. This book rings with a call to those who want to do more than merely bemoan the fate of humanity. It beckons to those who seek to understand the divine purpose in the deployment of God's sovereign wisdom and power, and to glimpse the loving presence that abides even through life's most horrendous journeys and seasons. Prepare for moments of tears, reflection, illumination, and perhaps even of heated debate. Recommended for all those who want to grapple with life's tough questions and are ready to exchange recycled platitudes for a true quest to hear God's voice and see his provision in the storm."

— Professor Peyi Soyinka-Airewele, Ithaca College, New York., USA

Behold, I Make All Things New!

Behold, I Make All Things New!

An Exploration of God's Goodness in Light of the Existence of Evil

'Tunde Agboola, PhD

ISBN: 979-8-9860256-1-2

Scripture quotations are from:

English Standard Version (ESV)
King James Version (KJV)
The Passion Translation (TPT)
New International Version (NIV)
Good News Translation (GBT)
New Living Translation (NLT)
Amplified Bible (AMP)
Amplified Bible, Classic Edition (AMPC)
Literal Standard Version (LSV)

Humbly dedicated to God, my wife Elizabeth Oyenike Agboola, my sons Toluwani David Agboola and Ayooluwa Daniel Agboola for weathering the storm with me as we navigated Ayanfeoluwa's health challenge together…and to my daughter Ayanfeoluwa Achsah Agboola, whose life and story inspired this book …and my father of blessed memory, Gabriel Atanda Agboola, who together with my mother Ruth Omobolanle Agboola laid the foundation for everything I have become today.

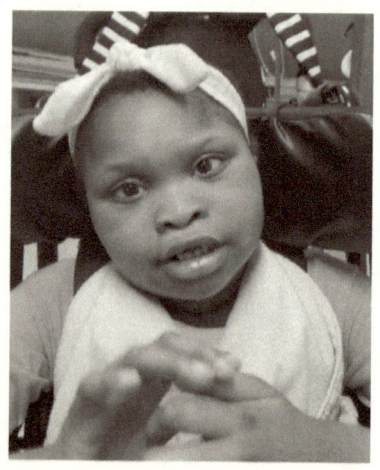

Ayanfeoluwa (picture taken on Easter Day — April 17, 2022)

Table of Contents

Preface

Behold, I Make All Things New! has a lot to say about the problem of evil and the rationalization that comes from perspective and experiences emanating from the love of and desire of both God and man to have children and sustain the child they love. If we seek to have, love and nourish our children, why would it be impossible for God to pursue the same since He created us? You will better under what I am saying when you read the rest of this book.

Solomon was one of the wisest men who ever lived. During his reign as King of Israel, two women approach him to help them resolve a dispute over who owns a living child. Both women had a child. One child is dead, and one is alive. The question was, who owns the living child? The story is in 1Kings 3:16-28. King Solomon pretended he would cut the child into two to resolve this conflict. One of the women could not stand having the child cut into two; the other, who was not the child's mother, said it was all right to kill the child. The mother of the child is the one who does not want him dead because of her unwavering love for the child. You see a pearl of effortless wisdom to identify who the child's mother was. She was okay giving the child to the other woman to keep the child alive than watching the child die because she unconditionally loved the child.

There is something in us all that would do anything to preserve and sustain the children we love, even if it means letting go and enduring a season of pain. Moses' mother is another example of this. Two additional examples are Mary the mother of Jesus and Joseph his father. If we can do this, how much more is God who said:

> ...Can a woman forget her own baby and not love the child she bore? Even if a mother should forget her child, I will never forget you. Jerusalem, I can never forget you! I have written your name on the palms of my hands. (Isaiah 49:15-16 GNT)

My experience of raising our beloved daughter, Ayanfe, with my wife inspired this book. Ayanfe was born with a genetic disorder, which led to my quest to understand and provide an intelligent and biblical explanation for the coexistence of evil, pain, and suffering and omnibenevolent, omnipotent, omniscient, omnipresent God.

The theme that runs throughout the book to justify God's allowance of evil is His love for His son Jesus and His desire to have children from among the children of men. The inspiration for this book was also my deep desire to make sense of the purpose of my daughter's genetic disorder considering my belief in a good God who formed her in my wife's womb. Insight was also provided using the process of childbirth to help make sense of the problem of evil and God's goodness.

There is a mystery in our desire to procreate and what we are willing to allow and endure to have, protect, preserve, and sustain our children. Therefore, if you have ever been a child or desired to have and raise children or understand why we do what we do to preserve our children, you have a better frame of mind to get the best out of this book. The words "Sons" and "Sonship" are used in the text in keeping with Biblical use, referring to both male and female humans.

The book seeks to provide a rational, intelligent, logical, and biblical response to the problem of evil and defend God's goodness. I write this book to inspire, support, and encourage all people, notably all followers of Jesus Christ who might be going through inexplicable pain and suffering and are questioning the goodness of God. However, the book's content will benefit atheists, agnostics, and unbelievers alike. The book will also help equip disciples of Jesus Christ to share and defend their belief in a good God.

Sincerely,

Dr. 'Tunde Caleb Agboola

June, 2022

Acknowledgments

This book is the product of a team of people; some have never met each other before. God connected me with many of His children who supported and helped make this book possible. I am grateful to God for all these brothers and sisters. Thank you all very much

The following people gave their time to listen to me share some of the content of this book in the early phase of development either through Zoom conversation or personally. Oloyede Odeyale, Kehinde Oladipupo, PhD., Michelle Board, Michael Ozegbe, Nick Werse, PhD., Daniel Miller, Jamie Lemon Norris, Jason Gregg, and Pst. Joshua Pancher. Thank you all for your feedback and comments and for encouraging me to move forward to complete this book. You all were my initial audience, and I am forever grateful.

Oloyede Odeyale, Kehinde Oladipupo, PhD., Rev. Damilola Abraham, Dayo Adeyemo, Nick Werse, PhD., Rev Doyle Bell, Vincent Engobor, Pst. Mike Cameneti, Pastor Butch Smith, Toyin Okelana, Sunday Oguntola, Tayo Akinola, Adeoye Adegorite, PhD., Michael Ozegbe, and Peyi Soyinka-Airewele, PhD., took the time to review the manuscript. They all provided beneficial feedback that improved the delivery of this book. I am eternally grateful for all your efforts and your friendship.

Thanks to Sunday Oguntola, my biological sister Remilekun Agboola, Adedunni Olayinka (née Adelakun), and Ademola Akinrinola, PhD., for proofreading the manuscript. I also want to thank my mother, Ruth Agboola, and my parents-in-law, Deacon. (Engr.) Samuel and Esther Oyedokun for their support. I am thankful to my father-in-law for connecting me with his friend – the CAN president.

My wife, Elizabeth Oyenike Agboola, gave herself to this work from conception to completion. She was very supportive from the initial discussion of writing this book to the writing of the manuscript and through the final review and proofreading of the book. In a sense, we co-authored this work together. Thank you, dear. I could not have asked for a better wife, friend, and help from the Lord.

Reverend. (Dr.) Supo Ayokunle, the president of the Christian Association of Nigeria (CAN), surprised me when he agreed to read the manuscript despite his hectic schedule. Thank you all so much.

Introduction

The book you are holding is not ordinary, not because I wrote it but because it was inspired and the weight of glory and presence, I felt the first time I read the rest of this introduction was very unusual. I was in tears and awe of God and felt so little and unworthy to write it. My understanding is that God has shown me mercy and chose to use me to convey His heart to my generation. This book has four sections:

Section 1 *"Rational defense for a good God"*, started with a brief story of my daughter that led to the writing of this book. Chapter Two is a very rational and introspective chapter, written to provide thorough and careful reasoning to justify the fact that God is good. The argument's premise came from a statement of Jesus Christ recorded in the Bible. To help atheists, agnostics, and non-believers reading the book find a reason to believe and better appreciate the discussion in Chapter 2, Chapters Three and Four focus on why there is a God and why we should rely on the Bible, respectively.

Section 2, *"Origin of evil and God's eternal purpose and desire"*, starts with Chapter Five that builds on Section one to address the origin of the manifestation of evil. In addition, Chapter Six provides a reason why God allows the expression of evil to continue despite His foreknowledge about the possibility of evil deeds. God's eternal purpose and desire that He must accomplish in time is the reason for which He allows evil to manifest in existence to date. God desires to have children (sons). Consequently, God gave Adam (before iniquity was also found in man) the dominion mandate to be fruitful, multiply, and replenish the earth by raising godly seeds. Chapter Seven is about what it means for God to have sons according to the Bible.

Section 3, *"God's plan against evil on Earth"*, focuses on demonstrating the active goodness of God. Although Section 2 seeks to exonerate God from evil, it might not be sufficient to support and demonstrate God's goodness. Section 3 addresses just that, beginning with Chapter Eight, to show that when God incarnated in the person of Jesus Christ, all he went about doing was good. Then Chapter Nine further strengthens the argument for the goodness of God through the continuation of Christ's good deeds by the body of Christ. Through the Holy Spirit, the body of Christ is the primary agent of goodness on the earth until the culmination of all things in the dispensation of the fullness of time. As though that is not good enough, Chapter Ten then explains God's goodness in setting up a system of human delegated authority to reward good and punish evil as part of His plan to contain evil deeds on the earth. In summary, Section 3 demonstrates God's inherent, present, and continuing goodness on the earth, hence God must be indeed good.

Section 4, "*Hope while making sense of the problem of evil*", begins with Chapter Eleven to answer the typical questions during pain and suffering like "Why do bad things happen to good people?" "Where was God when this or that was happening?" "If God is all-powerful and good, why is He not answering my prayers?" etc.

Having answers to those questions is excellent, but that might not change our expectation for a change of state from pain and suffering to bliss. Chapter Twelve gives a powerful biblical exposition on the hope in the certainty of the promise of God. All situations can change, and several will change as God promised when all conditions have aligned. However, there will be some situations that in God's eternal wisdom might remain; it is to such people and all of us who have experienced pain and suffering in any capacity that Chapter Thirteen speaks. We are all encouraged to keep hope alive because God will make all things new as promised, and He cannot lie!!!

The different sections of this book may appeal to different readers. So feel free to start reading from whatever section appeals most to you. It is important to note that Chapter Two of this book will require careful and thoughtful reading. If you find it difficult, a synopsis is provided towards the end of Chapter Six.

I commend this book to the able hand of God - the Father, Son, and the Holy Spirit. I trust Him to speak to you through the pages of this book and His words in the pages. I will strongly encourage you to read this book thoughtfully, carefully, and prayerfully. It is all right to take a break to think, meditate and prayerfully seek God's face through every page. You will get the best out of this book in that way. Below is my prayer as I release this book:

> Father in Heaven, I pray that You will bless this "Five loaves and two fishes" of mine to feed all souls that read. Let it minister grace to all. I commend this book to your able hands, Father, and the heart of all readers.

SECTION 1

RATIONAL DEFENSE FOR A GOOD GOD

Introduction

Chapter One

How It All Began

A Father's Quest

It all began on the fateful Wednesday afternoon of December 12, 2012. My wife and I went for a regular obstetrician appointment. We were expecting a baby girl. I believed God had promised me the birth of an extraordinary girl that I would name Achsah, the daughter of Caleb—a name that I acquired at my baptism.

When we got to the doctor's office, he asked for something that we had forgotten to bring to the appointment. So he asked me to get it from home. I left expecting to come back and hear the good news of the plan toward our baby's birth—the pregnancy was thirty-six weeks and five days. Thirty-seven weeks would be considered full term. While at home, I got a phone call that the doctor had moved my wife to College Station Medical Center, the main hospital, for immediate delivery of the baby. Our daughter's oxygen saturation level was getting lower than expected (oxygen desaturation). The doctor had told us about this earlier and that my wife needed rest, which she did. My wife had a fibroid, which the doctor thought might be affecting the baby. He had previously sent us to a specialist. The specialist had confirmed that everything was fine with the baby—essentially everything looked normal.

When my wife got to the main hospital, the medical staff performed an ultrasound check immediately. The result showed that our baby's head measured the expected size for thirty-four weeks while the body was showing thirty-six weeks.

A doctor carried out a C-section to deliver the baby because of this new information about desaturation and potential abnormal development. Her birth by C-section was on December 13th, 2012, the day after what we thought would be a routine appointment.

She looked healthy at birth, but she had an umbilical hernia. After I saw her, took pictures, and enjoyed being a very proud and happy dad, they took her to the neonatal ICU to check that everything was medically all right. Hours later, one of the doctors told us that our daughter was passing out due to rapid oxygen desaturation. Therefore, they needed to fly her out to Texas Children's Hospital—it was an emergency.

A Hopeless Situation—Where Was God and His Goodness in This?

After some medical tests at Texas Children's Hospital, we found out that she has a genetic anomaly called Chromosome 18-q deletion. It was a distal deletion—one of the long arms of the eighteen pairs of chromosomes had been deleted. The consequences of this genetic anomaly, whose cause is not known to date, include gross developmental delay, a hole in the heart, respiratory issues, and the like. When I was writing this book, she turned nine, but she still cannot sit independently, stand, walk, or speak intelligible words, although she can identify our voices and see. Her mental capacity and function are still like a baby younger than six months old. Since then, we have been taking care of her with nearly 24-hour attention. Recently, we got some additional help.

This seemingly hopeless situation brought frustration and pain to us. On top of this, we also have two healthy boys to take care of and ensure they live to the fullest. The pain and suffering of that experience aggravated us as it naturally robbed us of vital relationships and community, even among believers. Besides, we lived in another country (USA), far from our country of birth, which meant we had no immediate family members to help us. My wife had to drop what she planned to achieve academically and career-wise to take care of our daughter. She now holds a master's degree in professional accounting. I was studying for my PhD. in aerospace engineering at Texas A&M University when she was born. She was admitted to Texas Children's Hospital for a month but still went home without the desaturation problem fixed. Imagine the stress, pain, suffering, tears, sorrow, and anxiety.

What makes this very painful, and confusing is that I have had the opportunity as a young man to see God do miracles and cast out devils from oppressed people. I have seen God heal convulsion; I have witnessed barrenness healed by God supernaturally and more. You can imagine that I prayed and fasted and reached out to men who I thought had power with God. All these attempts did not change anything about my daughter's health. I experienced disappointments, dashed hopes, and the nothingness of the *best* of every man of God in and of themselves. My big question was "How does God's goodness fit with a genetic disorder, given Psalm 139:13–18?"

> You created every part of me; you put me together in my mother's womb. I praise you because you are to be feared; all you do is strange and wonderful. I know it with all my heart. When my bones were being formed, carefully put together in my mother's womb, when I was growing there in secret, you knew that I was there—you saw me before I was born. The days allotted to me had all been recorded in your book before any of them ever began. O God, how difficult I find your thoughts; how many of them there are! If I counted them, they would be more than the grains of sand. When I awake, I am still with you. (GNT)

The issue in one's mind is that there must be an explanation. I had a couple of thoughts about the possible cause and the difficulty those plausible explanations posed to my mind and that of an average person:

1. The first is the child's sin and the parents' sin.
2. God is evil, so He decided to form the child with a disorder.
3. The parent lacked faith in God.
4. The Devil caused it.
5. God is good, but He has less power than the Devil who caused it.
6. It is just because we live in a broken world.
7. God is good, but He is weaker than the broken world.

So this brought me to a hard road of asking the same question I have seen many people ask: "Where was God when this was happening?" I thought the Bible said He formed my daughter in my wife's womb. I thought He said He loved us, and He is good. I thought all the promises of God were yes and amen! If all of these were true and I have prayed, fasted, and sought help with men of God in humility, why was God not healing my daughter? Why was God distant and quiet?

My wife and I thought maybe we had sinned, so we repeatedly asked for mercy and forgiveness. Yet nothing changed. You can imagine how this might potentially weaken our faith and commitment to God and the scriptures. My experience with God was so real that I found the strength somehow by His grace to continue in my commitment to Jesus and His ways. However, the reality of the questions on the problem of evil were now so palpable for me. I could no longer ignore it. I couldn't avoid it with faith talk or positive thinking. I would have had to deny the obvious to ignore that question both by me and others I have encountered over the years. The question of dealing with the coexistence of a good, benevolent God in light of inexplicable pain, suffering, hardship, and evil now became a challenge for me to resolve.

Personally, it seems I have developed a way to deal with the pain about my daughter's health challenges. I feel anyone with similar or worse experiences would agree with me that it is apparent that we can no longer ignore the challenge of the problem of evil and the benevolence of God. There must be a way to rationalize the issue, and I needed to find out.

A New Book Is Born

I felt the need to seek personal understanding and make sense of the problem of evil and the benevolence of God when I put together the story of our daughter's birth, the unexpected death of my father in 2018, close to when I thought I was now able to start repaying him for training and investing in me—ensuring that I was formally educated and knew the Lord, with the myriad questions college students in America have asked me as I've shared the gospel, and other bad experiences I have had. However, my final decision to write about it did not come until 2020, when God spoke to me from Revelation 21:5 (GNT) "Then the one who sits on the throne said, 'And now I make all things new!' He also said to me, 'Write this, because these words are true and can be trusted.'"

The first event that led to this book occurred when I listened to a pastor preach about theodicy (the vindication of divine goodness and providence in light of the existence of evil) at a church I once attended in 2017. I was a small group leader in the church, and that week we were supposed to discuss the sermon in the small group. At that point, I realized I needed to have my response to theodicy.

The morning of the small group, during my time alone with God, I prayed for insight and revelation to help me and other group members resolve the question of theodicy: "God, you need to tell me something because I need it for better walk with You. You can see my daughter here. She is sick, and I have done everything in my power to seek miraculous intervention and medical solutions and all to no avail." My complaint to God that morning was "Although I am aware that we could try to cope and deal with this through prayer, counseling, which we have tried to do, there has to be a rational explanation." I wrestled with the question of why this kind of evil, pain and suffering exists in the first place, considering

God's existence. I pondered why, if God created everything, formed my daughter in my wife's womb, saw her unformed substance, and He is all-powerful and good, she was born with the disorder. I also prayed with my wife for the Holy Spirit to grant us insight that morning. While I was praying with my wife, a scripture popped into my spirit. I knew it was the Holy Spirit. I do believe the Holy Spirit speaks. The Holy Spirit brought a saying of Jesus Christ expressed in two scripture verses to my heart. I decided to go look them up. That text of scripture formed the axiom behind my rationalization of the problem of evil.

I must say at this stage that, for me, the issue of the problem of evil was not so much the existence of evil. Evil does exist, and any sincere human would admit that—period! The way I joke about this if someone says to me there is no evil in the world is to imagine someone slapping or punching that person in the face —on the spot, that person will come to terms with the reality of evil.

If we follow the obvious question to its root cause, the ultimate challenge for me was a first cause issue. The question was "How in the first place did evil exist if God existed, created the world, and is all-powerful, all-knowing, omnipresent, and good?" In other words, how could a good God have created *everything*, and yet evil exist? In my opinion, these are expressions of the fundamental question of theodicy!

Right off the bat, let me make it clear that I was learning this truth and grappling with it as a Christian, not a skeptic or an atheist. I already believed that God is good and benevolent. According to the claim of scripture, I had already believed that God is omnipotent, omnipresent, and omniscient. So as you read this book, it is all right for you to have that *fact* in your mind. Therefore, I am writing to rationalize and *defend* the claim that an all-powerful, all-knowing, omnipresent, benevolent, and good God exists concurrently with evil. In other words, the existence of such a good God and the existence of evil are not mutually exclusive.

This book aims to help skeptics believe and encourage believers to increase faith in the God they have already accepted. Therefore, some parts of this book include rationalization to help the skeptic overcome the logical barrier against belief. Other sections of the book involve assisting believers in making sense of the problem of evil by considering the revelation of scriptures they already believe. In addition, some parts include words of encouragement, motivation, and hope to anyone currently going through specific pain and suffering in their lives. Finally, I hope to provide a big picture of God's current and ultimate plan to eradicate evil. I pray that you will develop the courage to diligently seek the help of our good God amid life's storms and find hope such that you never live in doubt of the goodness of God.

Chapter Two

Rationalization of the Problem of Evil

God Alone is Good

Welcome to a rational world! This chapter is very mentally engaging and reflective. I encourage you to go through the mental exercise with me. Please do not jump to another chapter or give up on me. As a reminder, what I am writing about in this book is related to what theologians often call theodicy and the "problem of evil."

Theodicy—What Does It Mean?

Theodicy (from Greek *theos*, "god," and *dikē*, "justice") is the explanation of why a perfectly good, almighty, and all-knowing God permits evil. The term means "justifying God." Theodicies and defenses are two forms of response to what is known in theology and philosophy as the problem of evil (Encyclopedia Britannica). Theodicy is a defense of God's goodness and omnipotence given the existence of evil (Merriam-Webster's dictionary). Theodicy seeks to answer the question of why a good God permits the manifestation of evil, thus resolving the issue of the problem of evil. According to Jill Graper Hernandez (Department of Philosophy and Classics, University of Texas), the age-old question of theodicy is "Is the existence of God consistent or compatible with the presence of suffering in the world?" (Introduction of Special Issue "Theodicy," *Religions*, 2018).

The contentions associated with theodicy then suggest that if there are pain, suffering, sorrow, evil, disaster, and calamities in our world, then:

1. God may be good, but He is not all-powerful.
2. God is all-powerful, but He is not good.
3. God is good and all-powerful, but He is limited in knowledge.
4. At best, God is good, all-powerful, and all-knowing but not omnipresent.
5. Consequently, if there is a God, He does not combine the attributes of being all-good, benevolent, loving, omnipotent, omnipresent, and omniscient.

To argue about the problem of evil, we need to have axioms as a premise for further reasoning and argument. What I mean is that if there is an argument about whether striking a wall with your hand will be painful or not, one axiomatic statement of that argument is "There is a wall that someone can strike." If there is no such proposition, then the statement of the argument itself falls apart, making it irrelevant and baseless. In a sense, an axiom is a statement that is taken to be true, serving as a premise or beginning point for further reasoning and arguments. It is in this sense that I use the word axiom.

God Alone Is Good

Firstly, I do not think the contention surrounding the problem of evil makes any sense whatsoever if we do not posit the following as axiomatic:

1. there could be a God, at least ideologically—we may disagree if He genuinely exists or disagree on God's nature or attribute if He exists.

2. There are such things as good, goodness, love, etc. by definition.
3. There are such things as evil, evilness, pain, suffering, calamity, disaster, etc. by definition.

If we disagree with the above statements, I think the question of theodicy or the problem of evil is irrelevant, and we can spend our time with something else. If a God could or does exist, the problem of evil then is that He could not be good in light of the existence of evil. Therefore, the main argument is against the goodness of God and, in the far extreme, could be stretched to assert that God is evil. The contention, therefore, is that the biblical God—who is good— does not exist. The problem of evil is not about whether God exists; the contention is that God is not good and does not have all the attributes mentioned in the definition of theodicy simultaneously. This chapter does not focus on arguing for God's existence; instead, it attempts to rationalize that God is good and that God must be good if God exists. I am not saying that the argument for the existence of God is not a hot topic or irrelevant. It is a separate question, and I will be dealing with that in the next chapter. Hang on, sit tight, and get ready for the journey.

Secondly, my axiom for arguing my position on the problem of evil is that "If God exists, He alone is good in His existence and all good derives from Him." I contend that holding this truth is consistent with making sense of the problem of evil. I hope to demonstrate the validity of that proposition in this chapter. The claim of the Bible supports the axiom. The supporting text of the Bible is Luke 18:9 and Mark 10:18, which I said the Holy Spirit gave me, in chapter one, to resolve this conundrum.

> And a ruler asked him, 'Good Teacher, what must I do to inherit eternal life?' And Jesus said to him, 'Why do you call me good? No one is good except God alone.' (Luke 18:18–19, ESV)

> And as he was setting out on his journey, a man ran up and knelt before him and asked him, 'Good Teacher, what must I do to inherit eternal life?' And Jesus said to him, 'Why do you call me good? No one is good except God alone.' (Mark 10:17–18, ESV)

I will recommend that you read Luke 18:18-19 from multiple translations to help bring out the different shades of meaning. One immediate reaction that could come from an average reader is to consider my choice of using a statement from the Bible to argue on the issue of theodicy as self-defeating since my argument might be based on the belief that the Bible is factual. I believe that such a reaction is tenable. However, I would respond by saying that using a statement from the Bible does not mean I have to think that the Bible is reliable for the statement to be true. But if the statement is true, it may give a measure of credibility to the Bible. I will address such concerns in two ways:

1. The first way I will address the objection to the premise of my argument is to argue for my belief in the Bible and why the Bible is a reliable book for life and godliness. That is the focus of Chapter 4.
2. The second way to address the objection is to examine the statement itself on its credibility of being axiomatic (for the sake of our argument) without regard to its source.

Reserving the Exclusive Right to the Word "Good" for God

Before I address the two points above, oblige me for a while to build on my proposed axiom.

Put together, all the different translations of the Bible statement above strongly suggest reserving the exclusive right of the word "good" for *God*. Therefore, another way to state my earlier proposition is that "God alone is (the exclusive definition of) good." We cannot have a universal definition of what (absolute) good is except we pin it on what transcends all cultures and the nuances of human diversity of opinion and thought. And the God of the Bible (who I am arguing is good) transcends all these differences. The God I am arguing for is the God I believe created everything in the first place. I am arguing for God, not "the god of the gaps." I am arguing for the God I believe is personal, immanent in creation but transcendent of creation. I am arguing for God, the uncaused cause of all that ever existed. He is the eternal God who created everything from nothing (ex nihilo). Therefore, if He exists, He exists before and separated in His existence from the universe (holy) yet constantly working within the universe. Good must be inherent in Him; otherwise, what is the initial source of good?

If you disagree with the statement "God alone is good", I request that you provide an alternative definition of good. I am almost sure that all your definitions will be subjective and limited to your perception of reality. And if your definition of that which is good is relative, then what I consider to be good you might consider evil and vice versa. It makes no sense to argue about the problem of evil if the definition of good is subjective and relative. Accepting a personal definition of good affirms that good and evil fundamentally depend on persons, culture, creed, and our unique psychological makeup and idiosyncrasies, which most likely have been influenced by anthropology, sociology, theology, etc. Therefore, it seems to me that for us to have any argument at all, we must at least agree to move on with the proposition that God must be the definition of good. And honestly, I do not see how else we could go forward with this argument.

The proposition that God must be the exclusive definition of good means that God was good before He created anything at all. He did not learn to be good. He alone is inherently good. God was good before He made anything. So goodness derives from God. That is my position. If you are strong in your opinion about the problem of evil and are about to drop this book because you think I am too dogmatic, I will request that you bear with me for a bit and keep on reading.

How Did Evil Even Become a Possibility If God Alone Is Good?

I identify a couple of relevant objections to my submission that God alone is good.

Objection 1: If God is good and created everything, how did evil come about? Since this God is omnipotent, omnipresent, omniscient, all good and benevolent to top it off, how then did evil come about, and how does it still exist to date? Was God unaware of evil coming forth, even if it came out of nothing? Was He powerless to stop evil? Should it be that He was ignorant of when evil suddenly came out of nothing? Perhaps He was powerless to deal with evil after evil had escaped His omniscience and omnipresence?

Objection 2: If we state that God alone is good, is it illogical to posit that God alone is evil as well?

I will wait till a little later to respond to objection 1. The problem with objection 2 is that if you posit that God alone is evil, you will have to argue for how good came about since God created everything. Furthermore, a consistent and corroborative argument will also be needed, like what you are about to read in the rest of this chapter. I plan to support the proposition that God alone is good. My argument will be logical and ultimately based on a framework that rests on a proper understanding of the Bible from the original language and text.

Consistent with the first objection above, I believe the critical issue to address is how evil came about in the first place. How did evil exist since God who created everything ex nihilo is good and only goodness exists in Him? I must admit that this question about the origin of evil is challenging. The difficulty here is that we are grappling with how the evil we know exists could be compatible with the existence of a good, omnipotent, omniscient, omnipresent, and benevolent God

34

who we claim created everything. In other words, it appears illogical that such a good God would make the world, and yet evil could exist.

Firmly stated, someone might say we would have to admit that the existence of evil and a good God is mutually exclusive and highly improbable. Such assertion may appear very solid and incontestable. However, I submit that the statement is not necessarily true after a second critical look. I attempt to falsify that claim of mutual exclusivity of the existence of a good God and the reality of evil. To prove that the claim is false, I must show that logically a situation or rationale could be conceived that allows for a good God to coexist with evil. The question now is: is there a conceivable logic consistent with the earlier proposition that falsifies the claim of mutual exclusivity of the existence of a good God and evil? My answer to that question is yes; that is the focus of the rest of this chapter.

Exclusivity of Good and God's Act of Creation— Why Evil Exists

Reserving the exclusive right to the word "good" for God makes rationalizing the problem of evil easier. However, I need to show that such an assumption holds. Saying that God alone is the definition of good means that *nothing* else is (essentially and truly) good apart from God. I conceive of an argument that if God alone is good and nothing else is good (not referring to goodness here, which derives from good), then anything else outside of God could be evil—not that it *must* be evil. Therefore, it is not illogical to state that if God created everything ex nihilo, then the existence of anything else outside of God could become what we now conceive of as evil. To make it more direct, my argument for the existence of evil mutually with a good God is that the moment or the fact that God decided to create and cause anything else to be apart from Himself made evil a possibility. Please note here that I am now dealing with the concept of the possibility of evil. I am not dealing with the perpetration, perpetuation, or manifestation of evil (which I define herein as evilness). I will discuss the perpetration and perpetuation later. It is expedient that I state here that the whole argument about evil being the inversion (or, loosely, the perversion) of God did not exist before creation. Before creation, there was only good because there was only God. After creation, we could now speak of good and evil (goodness and evilness) because something else apart from God existed after creation.

One way to make sense of my theory, which I call the asymptotic view of theodicy, is to use a basic analogy to analytical geometry. An asymptote is a line or curve that acts as the limit of another line or curve. For example, a descending curve that approaches but does not reach the horizontal axis is said to be asymptotic to that axis. That axis is the asymptote of the curve. In analytical geometry, a line that continually approaches a given curve but does not meet it at any finite distance is considered an asymptote.

I see good and evil in that sense of an asymptote for everything or anything that God created, which means that anything *created* could tend to the asymptote of evil or good. And since I define God alone as good, it logically follows that when God (who is good) does not influence anything created, that thing could asymptotically tend toward evil. This tendency towards evil is what I call evilness. The movement to the asymptote of good is what I envision as goodness. A great example of an asymptote is the mathematics of inverse or reciprocal. A reciprocal is a multiplicative inverse. An example of an inverse function is $y = 1/x$. The curve of $1/x$ is in figure 1. The asymptotes are the horizontal and vertical axes. Please note that this illustration is just for pedagogy and not a complete picture of the truth claim. Having stated this, let us continue making sense of this asymptotic theory.

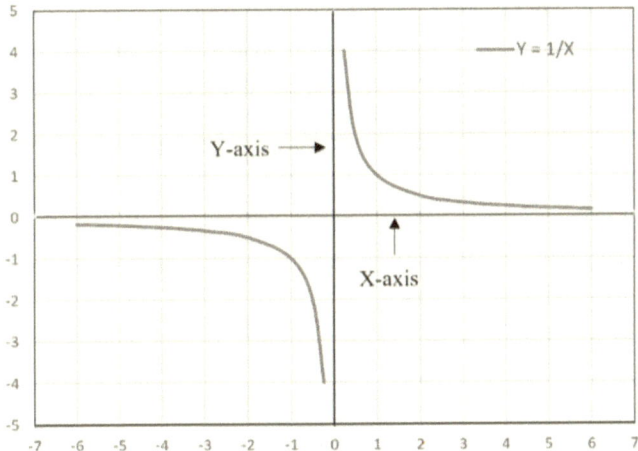

Figure 1: A plot of 1/x showing asymptotes.

In keeping with the analogy, think of good as the x-axis (and we state that good is God) and consider the y-axis as evil. The positive quadrant is all of existence. And the curve is the line where all conscious existence lived. Just as y = 1/x, in a limited sense for illustration, evil is only a derivative of good when good is "inverted" or corrupted. Before anything existed, good was the independent variable. Absolute evil, just like y, derives from good (x) as an inverse. Therefore, we could not conceive evil as anything (I daresay anyone) existing before creation in the same way we define good as God other than as a logical possibility. Based on the theory put forward in this book, we would have to conceive of an entity that predates the universe that could be the inverse of God for absolute evil to be defined. However, we could practically describe evil as evilness being a derivate of goodness. Therefore, within this framework, when it comes to absolute evil, I contend that we could only think of it as an abstract concept in the sense that God could have an inversion. Pre-creation, only good existed since God alone existed. Post-creation, good exists as goodness and evil exists as evilness. When I discuss evil in post-creation reality, I refer to evilness, just like when I think of good, I am dealing with goodness in post-creation fact.

Clearly stated, good is that which exists before creation because God is good, and God alone existed before God created anything. Evil would only be a derivative of good as the corruption of good, not necessarily that which is not good. If evil is the same as "not good," we would have to consider everything else as evil outside of God to be consistent. The concept here is that whenever God creates anything, it falls within the space bounded by the x (good) and y (evil) axis, so it is neither absolute good nor complete evil. However, such a thing can tend toward good or evil in the extremum. The potential energy for the tendency toward good or evil is consciousness, and the driving force is desire. The desire of a conscious being is the driving force for good or evil. Therefore, anything that God created that is not conscious can only be amoral (neutral) by default, and only conscious beings have the potential to drive things toward good or evil.

Essentially, anything that is not conscious or has desire stays neither good nor evil (like the stars, trees, and inanimate things) except when God says it is good—when God says it, it is. However, conscious beings with a desire can act in manners that tend asymptotically toward good or evil. Therefore, we cannot call anything good by its existence other than God. Think of all created entities' initial condition or state as amoral (neutral). Depending on the driving force, the final state of existence is either good or evil. If God's desire is the driving force, it will tend toward good (God). Otherwise, it stays amoral (neutral). But as we will state later in this book, another being became the Devil (I sometimes just say he is the "doer of **evil**"). Hence, his selfish desire became the driving force for evilness. He is the entity closer to (absolute) evil, although he is not absolute evil. He is the first perpetrator of evil. This entity is the closest you can get to when conceiving the concept of the inverse of God (which is called evil). By implication, we will see that humans also inherited that selfish desire at the fall of Adam and Eve. Human selfish desire has now become another driving force for the perpetration and perpetuation of evil.

Goodness or evilness as the reality of good and evil is only due to the potential it inherits from conscious beings and the driving force it inherits from the desire of conscious beings. This theory is supported by James 4:1–2 (TPT):

> Where do all the fights and quarrels among you come from? They come from your **desires** for pleasure, which are constantly fighting within you. You want things, but you cannot have them, so you are ready to kill; you **strongly desire** things, but you cannot get them, so you quarrel and fight. You do not have what you want because you do not ask God for it.

This concept of the potential and driving force for goodness and evilness is so powerful that it is a significant contribution to understanding many of the realities that make us cast aspersion on God and attribute evil to Him. I daresay ahead of time, as we will see when we start discussing the perpetration and perpetuation of evil, that selfish desire is the driving force for evilness, and God-given desire is the driving force for all-around goodness. And that overall goodness is motivated by love. And love is of God, and those who love are born of God. In other words, all-around goodness is born from and of God's desire.

In Genesis chapter 1, the Bible records the creation of the universe. One repeated phrase is "And God saw that it was good." It is as though God, a conscious entity with the potential and desire as a driving force for good, was watching that all He created tended toward His good purpose for creation. And each time, He only allowed that thing to stay in existence when it drove toward good. That act of God shows not only that God is good but demonstrates His goodness. He actively works all things toward good (which is Himself, His consciousness, and His desire):

Romans 8:28—"And we know that for those who love God all things work together for good, for those who are called according to his purpose."

Ephesians 1:11—"In him, we have obtained an inheritance, having been predestined according to the purpose of him who **works all things** according to the counsel of His will."

I want to clarify that this asymptotic analogy is for limited illustration and pedagogy. If we consider the analogy as the actual reality, it might lead to an erroneous conclusion. For example, is God, then, on a line and has a different degree of Himself as we could conceive the different magnitude of the number on the x-axis and, by implication, all that follows with it? The answer is *no*; that is not the purpose of this illustration.

Didn't God Create Evil?

At this point, I consider it reasonable to note that the Bible did state that God created or does evil. Confirm this assertion in the following scriptures:

> Isaiah 45:7 (KJV)—"I form the light, and create darkness: I make peace, and create evil: I the LORD do all these things."

> Amos 3:6 (KJV)— "Shall a trumpet be blown in the city, and the people not be afraid? Shall there be evil in a city, and the LORD hath not done it?"

The Hebrew word used for "create" in Isaiah 45:7 is the word *bara* (H1254 in *Strong's Concordance*). It is the same word used for "create" in Genesis 1:1: "In the beginning, God created [bara] heaven and the earth." In that scriptural text, the Hebrew word used for evil is *rah* or *raw-aw* (H7451 in *Strong's Concordance*). It is the same word used for "evil" in Genesis 2:17: "But you must not eat from the tree of the knowledge of good and evil, for when you eat from it you will certainly die."

This assertion of the Bible creates a little challenge for us as it seems that God is the creator or cause of evil. How does that not prove that God cannot be considered good? We can't make that conclusion because at least one scripture suggests there is *no evil in God* but that all good and perfect gifts come from Him – the father of light:

> Psalm 92:15 (NLT)—"They will declare, 'The LORD is just! He is my rock! There is **no evil in him!**'"

> Psalm 5:4 (LSV)—"For You [are] not a God desiring wickedness, **Evil does not inhabit You.**"

> James 1:13–18 (ESV)—"…for **God cannot be tempted with evil,** and he himself tempts no one. But each person is tempted when he is **lured and enticed by his own desire…Every good gift and every perfect gift is from above, coming down from the Father of lights…**"

> Mark 7:21–23 (TPT) —" **Evil originates from inside a person…All these corrupt things emerge from within** …

Combining these scriptures leads to an excellent puzzle for sure! The later set of scriptures affirms that God has no evil in him and that evil originates from within. Therefore, if God has no evil in him, evil could not have originated from Him. On the other hand, the earlier set of scriptures suggests that God creates or does evil. There seems to be tension between the former and later sets of scriptures. However, one way to align these scriptural verses is to state that God did not conceive evil and craft it into existence as His desire. Someone might argue inconsistency with the scripture here.

Nevertheless, in the light of my argument in this book, I do not see inconsistency with that scripture and the assertion that God alone is good. I think that statement is true in light of the argument I have put forward so far. I am sure you are wondering what I mean. I mean, if God alone is good, and He decided to create *anything* apart from Himself, it would not be illogical to state that God "created" evil as a subset of the fact that He made *everything* that ever existed. We cannot say that God conceived of evil to bring it to pass as we will design and develop a car or an airplane. But we could imagine that statement in the sense that we speak of a car manufacturing company as causing or creating all car accidents. If there were no cars, there would have been no car accidents. It is interesting how this kind of allegation happens every day. I spoke with a friend in the litigation department of an automotive component manufacturing company. He told me how people had sued the company for causing injury to them because they were driving a car that included a component manufactured by his company.

In that sense, we cannot logically rule out the assertion that evil exists because God created everything, and evil is a thing. Consequently, God created evil. Yet we must restate that God did not create evil (cause evil to exist) as a plan He primarily conceived. The possibility of evil logically can be attributed to God making anything in the first place. Who cares about evil if it does not cause pain, suffering, death, mourning, and loss? I imagine we couldn't care less about evil if it is not acted out or perpetrated. Would we even discuss evil except that whatever we call evil has an undesirable consequence on humans?

> Then came there unto him all his brethren, and all his sisters, and all they that had been of his acquaintance before and did eat bread with him in his house: and they bemoaned him, **and comforted him over all the evil that the LORD had brought upon him**: every man also gave him a piece of money, and everyone an earring of gold. (Job 42:11 KJV)

This verse in the book of Job perfectly illustrates my point. According to this verse, it was written that the Lord brought evil upon Job. However, if you read the book of Job from chapter 1, you will see that the Lord did not bring evil upon Job. Satan brought evil upon Job, although God allowed it for a greater purpose. So when we read that God created or did evil, it is in this sense that I believe the scripture is speaking.

If you follow my logical build-up, you should be expecting me to deal with rationalizing the perpetration of evil within this framework knowing that God exists and He is still alive and has always been alive and Omnipotent. You may ask, "Why did He not prevent evil from being perpetrated and perpetuated?" You may believe that is a bigger problem. It appears the perpetration of evil is a bigger fish to fry, but there is a conceivable explanation for why God would have allowed the perpetration of evil. God is *all-powerful* to stop evil. He is *all-knowing* to know that evil will be perpetrated or perpetuated. He is present everywhere (omnipresent), such that He will see evil about to be performed even if evil wanted to come through the back door. Why was there evilness in the first place?

The Perpetration and Perpetuation of Evil

The question or issue in this section is how God's creation (God being good and created all things) tends toward evil or is used to perpetrate or perpetuate evil. We have stated earlier that the asymptote of all created things is either good or evil. We also noted that consciousness is the potential energy for good or evil and that the desire of any conscious being is the driving force for goodness and evilness.

According to the new world encyclopedia, "Consciousness, at its simplest, is sentience or awareness of internal or external existence. Despite millennia of analyses, definitions, explanations, and debates by philosophers and scientists, consciousness remains puzzling and controversial, being at once the most familiar and most mysterious aspect of our lives. Perhaps the only widely agreed notion about the topic is the intuition that it exists." So if all God created were nonconscious entities, there couldn't have been evil. However, as soon as God decided to make conscious (that is, self-aware) entities—creatures that could conceive of the notion of "I and other," evil already had potential energy!

43

I must bring this truth home at this point. Think about all the things you could consider evil today. It all originates when someone puts "I" first or thinks of "I" alone—selfish desire. In other words, self-awareness is the potential for evil, while selfish desire is the driving force for evilness. Think deeply about this. As you will see when I talk about the first perpetration of evil, it will be apparent that self-desire is the driving force for evil, and that principle runs throughout history.

According to the testimony of the Bible, the first consciousness that God created that had a desire that led to the first perpetration of evil is the person the Bible calls Lucifer, who later became Satan, the Devil, the dragon, the serpent, etc. (see the Book of Revelation 12:1–17, ESV).

Based on the perspective provided in this book, an essential fact of the problem of evil is that so long as an alternative desire exists apart from God's, evilness as a reality will continue. Essentially, I am saying that the Bible or Christian approach to the problem of evil (theodicy) will only make sense if the Bible can explain how the desire of conscious beings will be eradicated or permanently and irrevocably constrained to God. And it seems to me that according to Matthew 25 and Revelation 21, God will judge the Devil and all evildoers in the lake of fire forever.

If consciousness is the potential for evil, will God then eradicate consciousness for evil to be no more? No!! However, in keeping with God's goodness, there will be a state of existence where the Bible says that the tabernacle of God will dwell with men (Revelation 21:3 (KJV)). That state of existence looks to me like God will put Himself and His desire within and around consciousness permanently so that both the potential energy and the driving force for evil are no more.

God will fill all things with Himself, His desire and love as a final wrap-up of the former things and the making of all things new after He has completed His plan to fulfill His desire to have sons. These sons are the overcomers who have conquered evil and will have an eternal inheritance as heirs of the Father (Revelation 21:5, 7)

Why Did God Create Anything If He Foreknew Evil Was Possible?

So far, we have argued for the existence of evil and the perpetuation of evil. However, we have significant difficulty with this view if we factor the foreknowledge of God into the equation. An average reader may pose the question, "If God knew evil was possible when He created anything outside of Himself, why did He not stop creating so that evil never existed at all since God is only good and does good only?" That is a legitimate question when we think of a good God's desire, who has foreknowledge. But before you say, "Case closed", let me put it to you that there is a possible and powerful answer to that question that is still consistent with this framework. The answer to that question is as follows:

1. God has a purpose and desire inherent to His existence, which He purposed in Himself before anything else (Psalm 51:6, Ephesians 1:9, Ephesians 1:5).
2. God wants and plans to fulfill His desire and purpose (Ephesians 1:10–11, Isaiah 46:9–11).
3. The possibility of evil could not have stopped an all-powerful God from fulfilling His desire and purpose (Isaiah 14:24, 26–27).
4. If the possibility of evil and the potential or driving force for the perpetration and perpetuation of evil could stop God from performing His desire and purpose, then evil is now more potent than God since it could stop God from doing what He wanted to do.
5. All the attributes and nature of God work together in all His decisions and actions. So for example, the goodness of God cannot deny His omnipotence in all the things He does or allows. This truth is a fundamental principle for

making sense of many things that we consider evil, which look like God brought or allowed.

To avoid confusion about my position, I state that I believe that God is never the source of evilness to anyone, but He does permit it sometimes. Whenever God allows what we see as evilness, it is because His attributes, desire, or purpose of His nature cannot disagree. But He is always working toward good during it all. We will discuss this much better in later chapters.

Considering the above responses, I propose that a desire and purpose of God that He must fulfill are the reasons He did not stop creation to prevent evil and evilness from existing. And I do not think it is inconceivable to say that God wants and will fulfill His desire and purpose if you and I do the same—He created us. Therefore, our desire to satisfy all our wants and purpose is not illogical because God Himself, who created us, has the same desire. *One might say that the passion and purpose of God stand as two of the possible things that could stop God from operating His power.* Essentially, the omnipotence of God is not that God can do anything; it is that God can do anything He desires to do within His purpose. For example, God cannot lie! By nature, lying is not in Him, nor is it His desire. Think of this principle as an illustration of the integrity of God. He cannot deny Himself in any of the things He does or allows. God is a single unified entity in all His attributes. Therefore, His Holiness, power, goodness, love, desire, and purpose act in congruence every time God does anything. *If God is not moving or acting in power, something in His personality or nature must be kept in balance and at the same level as His power.* Otherwise, God would have to deny Himself to show or prove that He was all-powerful. This principle I am laying out is fundamentally and extremely useful as we later look at several stories in the Bible where it seems as though God lacked the power to stop evil.

I also want to state clearly that every time evil appears to be having a field day, it is not because God is powerless, indifferent, or uncaring. *God is working to create the necessary condition that allows Him to act in unity with all His attributes to eradicate evil in time and ultimately forever.* What desire and purpose motivated God to create if/when He foreknew that evil and evilness could be? That is what I will discuss in chapter 6.

The argument made so far is to help the skeptics and the rationally minded people come along on this journey. From here forth, I want to state categorically that my argument is on the bedrock of the Christian worldview. I do not hide that this is a book by a Christian who presents an argument consistent with the Christian worldview. I believe it is only in the Christian worldview that I could consistently answer the question of the problem of evil in a manner that is consistent and corroborates with reality. When I speak of God from this point, I mean the God of Abraham, Isaac, and Jacob, the Father of our Lord Jesus Christ. Therefore, when I talk of desire and purpose, I speak of the desire and purpose of God as revealed in the Bible. The God who spoke His mind in the scriptures through human vessels by the Holy Spirit (2 Timothy 3:16–17, 2 Peter 1:20–21).

The rest of this book will be Bible based and stay consistent with the propositions and arguments I have built up to this point.

Chapter Three

There Is a God

Something from Nothing

P~salm~ 19:1–4 (ERV):

> The heavens tell about the glory of God. The skies announce what his hands have made. Each new day tells more of the story, and each night reveals more and more about God's power. You cannot hear them say anything. They don't make any sound we can hear. But their message goes throughout the world. Their teaching reaches the ends of the earth. The sun's tent is set up in the heavens.

Consider also this quote from Robert Boyle, the father of modern chemistry: "From the knowledge of God's work, we shall know Him."

In chapter 2, I stated that arguing about the problem of evil and the goodness of God would be baseless without the possibility of the existence of a God. In this chapter, I attempt to provide a reason to believe that there is a God. One of the many approaches to prove or disprove is the scientific approach. It is imperative to know that science can neither prove nor disprove the existence of God. Proving that God exists is above the realm of scientific theory. God is not observable, measurable, repeatable, and you cannot put God in a controlled environment. Above all, is the existence of God falsifiable? Scientifically, it is infinitely difficult if not nearly impossible to falsify a claim that God exists. You would have to have all knowledge and have been in all places and have all power to make all things be at your disposal to satisfy the scientific falsifiability requirement for the claim of the existence or nonexistence of God. Simply put, if there is a God, could God be living in Antarctica in the very heart of the ice? Perhaps He resides inside the black hole: "Then Solomon said, 'The LORD has said that he would **dwell in thick darkness**" (1 Kings 8:12). Or perhaps He lives at the core of the sun at about twenty-seven million degrees Fahrenheit: "Who alone has immortality, who dwells in **unapproachable light**, whom no one has ever seen or can see. To Him be honor and eternal dominion. Amen" (1 Timothy 6:16).

How would you either know that or falsify the claim? What if God is constantly moving faster than the speed of light from location to location yet leaving His presence everywhere He has ever been before? How do you falsify that claim? You would have to be able to move at the speed of light yourself at least. I am saying that we can only provide plausible logic that removes mental barriers against the likelihood that God exists.

However, science can lead you to a point where believing there is a God is more reasonable than disbelieving. The works of God's hand can help guide you to Him. To get you started on the path that might lead to the top of the mountain of reasoning, to see clearly and make a leap of faith that there is a God, I will provide a couple of concepts for your consideration in this chapter. Perhaps the facts presented may help you offload many of the rational mental barriers you might have built up against the existence of a creator of the cosmos or universe.

Similar concepts to some of those expressed in this chapter are present in many existing books by theologians and philosophers worldwide. I present some unique perspective in addition to a collection of relevant facts and resources from pre-existing knowledge in such a way that will help you think through the critical and life-defining question of the existence of a creator—God. I believe that the experience of God can only happen by faith, according to Hebrews 11:1, 6:

> Now faith is the assurance that what we hope for will come about and **the certainty that what we cannot see exists**…Without faith, no one can please God. Whoever comes to God must **believe that he** is real and that he rewards those who sincerely try to find him (emphasis added).

As soon as you believe, it is like your sixth sense awakens and you can see now that God exists. Open your eyes to see what you did not know was there all along because your eyes were closed. God must be revealed and apprehended by faith. As you may see from my thought process, God has revealed Himself in the Holy Bible through His Spirit and in creation. When you believe that He exists based on His handiworks and His revelations in the Bible, you will get to know Him, precept upon precept, line upon line, a little here and a little there. Since God is limitless, according to the Bible, we cannot exhaust knowing and understanding Him. He is new every morning and fresh every time!

As a precursor to defending the existence of a good, benevolent God considering the presence of evil, I hope to present short reasoning for the existence of God. Let's do just that!

The Most Probable Nature of the Creator: a Conscious Being

Humans are a part of the universe, and our very existence is a huge pointer to the possibility of a creator, at least the creator of humans. Therefore, if you and I exist and are rational, we cannot rule out the notion that a mind possibly created the universe.

My experience in life tells me that when you start to ask the question, "who created me?" the answer leads you to the conclusive end of the first uncaused cause of everything. A question every great thinker cannot ultimately ignore is this: "Is there an uncaused cause of everything – a creator?" Another follow-up question then is, "Is the creator a conscious being— a rational mind—or just a nonconscious entity?" The subsequent step will be to determine if your inclination of the type of entity the creator is makes sense considering that the creation has both conscious rational minds and nonconscious entities. We must reason:

1. Is it more likely that conscious beings like us come from some unconscious entities, or
2. Is it more likely that conscious beings created unconscious entities?

I propose that we determine the most logical position based on our current observation of reality. If the universe has conscious and unconscious entities, what is the most logical nature of the creator—conscious beings or lifeless entities? These questions are easy to deal with using the standard logic that scientists use every day. And the reasoning is to utilize observable phenomena to explain unobservable ones. Suppose we could show an example of current events where unconscious things came from conscious beings. In that case, we can at least theorize the possibility that a conscious creator created lifeless entities. On the other hand, if we have an example of observable phenomena where conscious, rational beings emerged from inanimate entities, we can also theorize that the creator could be a lifeless entity. In essence, do we have an example today where unconscious things were brought to existence by conscious beings and vice versa?

The most plausible of the two sides of this question is that consciousness creates unconscious entities. You, me, and all humans are conscious rational beings, and we make nonconscious things like cars, toys, laptops, mobile phones, food, fridges, etc.—just look around you. Therefore, it would make sense to me then that the creator of the universe is most likely a conscious entity than an unconscious entity. You are more *unlikely* to find in our present experiences where lifeless entities brought about conscious rational entities. Some scientists, trying to demonstrate that life could come from nonliving entities, have realized that it is an arduous task. It is tough and almost impossible as of today to explain or recreate how the first and simplest lifelike microscopic organisms (microbes) could have come from nonliving chemicals (abiogenesis). A very solid book that speaks to scientific opinions on the origin of life from non-life is *"the Mystery of Life's Origin – the Continuing Controversy"* by Charles B. Thaxton, Walter L. Bradley, Roger L. Olsen, and others.

Based on the above logic, if there is a creator of the universe, the entity is most likely a conscious rational being. I could not conceive that if there is a creator, the entity is a thing with no life or consciousness.

Is It Reasonable That God Could Exist?

The next thing we must convince ourselves of is the existence of a creator who is most likely a conscious being. Let me deal with this issue using a reverse argument, and it is a straightforward but profound one. You might wonder what that is. It is the thought that if there is no creator, how did the universe exist? You will have to deal with that heart-pounding question! At least to the best of your knowledge, everything you know comes from something, that comes from something, that comes from something. Following that logic to its reasonable conclusion, you will see that it is more logical to conclude that there must be something or someone from where everything else originated. To challenge this simple thought, I believe, is to begin a journey of endless questions, some of which might sound foolish. No wonder the Bible says, "The fool says in his heart, 'There is no God.' They are corrupt, doing abominable iniquity; there is none who does good" (Psalm 53:1 ESV).

52

Some highly respected scientists have made statements or have explored ideas that appear very confusing as they grapple with the concept of a creator. Some atheists have found solace in the idea of multiple universes as though the same problem does not exist even if there are multiple universes. The same question would be what caused the multiple universes to be?

One statement that has continued to baffle me is "Because there is a law such as gravity, the universe can and will create itself from nothing" (Stephen Hawking in the book *The Grand Design*). Is gravity nothing? Or to make it simpler, does gravity exist outside of the universe for gravity to have caused the universe to create itself? And how can the universe create itself? The question then is the origin of gravity. At best, you may postulate that gravity is the uncreated creator. I have argued earlier that it seems inconsistent with our present knowledge, and therefore most unlikely to be accurate, that the creator would be a lifeless entity like gravity. The creator is most likely a conscious being. The other option is to state that gravity is a conscious entity. If gravity is a conscious being, what was the whole issue with there being a God—the creator? God could as well be "Mr. Conscious Gravity."

You might be thinking this argument about something coming from something is considerably basic and straightforward. Yes, that is the point. It is not that difficult to know that God, the creator, exists. If God exists, He created you. If you exist, God could exist. No matter how advanced a professor of mathematics is, he cannot outgrow the basic math of $1 + 1 = 2$. He must not violate that in all complex calculations he/she does. In the same way, we can invent advanced ways, tools, instruments, and complicated logic to prove that God exists. My submission is that the ultimate question and final reasoning will still return to the basics: I exist. I am conscious. I can create. Who or what created me? Thinking through that question will most likely lead you to find the answer in one way or the other. It should begin from there.

Think about it! All these questions matter because you exist, and you are conscious.

The question to ask yourself is are you a conscious rational being? Do you think it is illogical to posit that a conscious being brought you to existence? From your direct knowledge of how things are created, a conscious being gave birth to you. Why would it be out of place to conceive of an ultimately uncaused conscious rational being that caused all life to come into existence? That uncaused conscious being that brought things into existence out of nothing (ex nihilo) is the one we call the creator—God.

Why There Being a God is Plausible—The Universe Has a Beginning

You might want to read books by Lee Strobel, Dr. Walter Bradley, Dr. Gerald Schroeder, Dr. Hugh Russ, Dr. William L. Craig, and many other apologists to gain more depth on this issue of there being a creator as their works helped me solidify much of the logic and many of the ideas expressed in this chapter. I know Dr. Walter Bradley personally. Walter is a mentor to me and taught me while I was a student at Baylor University. When the going was getting tough, He was incredibly supportive during my pursuit of a PhD. in aerospace engineering from Texas A&M University. Upon researching work compiled by these men, I found some essential truths that I want to summarize in this chapter.

Scientists have been observing creation for centuries and have come up with theories of the origin of the universe. If it is true that creation points to God, according to Psalm 19:1–4, then, scientific observation should ultimately confirm it. Let's see what the prevalent scientific view on the origin of the universe says about the likelihood of a creator.

The science field that studies the origin and development of the universe is called cosmology. The fundamental question of cosmology is "How did the universe begin?" There are several theories and views on the origin of the universe. I highlight two of the common ones as follows:

1. *Steady-State Theory*: From ancient times, the universe has been considered eternal. Essentially, the universe is timeless and has always remained and looked as it does today. This view of the universe is called the steady-state theory of the universe. It was challenged in the late 1950s when the big bang theory began to surface, stating that the universe started in a finite time in the past. The theory was first put forward in 1948 by British scientists Sir Hermann Bondi, Thomas Gold, and Sir Fred Hoyle. It was further developed by Hoyle to deal with problems that had arisen in connection with the alternative big-bang hypothesis.

2. *Big Bang Theory*: I once listened to Dr. Walter Bradley state that this theory's name was initially given as a mockery by those who hold to the steady-state theory. The big bang theory, in essence, is derived from the combination of the conclusions from Einstein's generalized theory of relativity and the observations of the Hubble Telescope. In Los Angeles in 1929, the Hubble Telescope showed that the galaxies are receding away from each other, suggesting that the universe is either in a dynamic state of contracting or expanding. The farther the galaxies' distance, the faster they recede away from Milky Way Galaxy. The Milky Way Galaxy is where the earth resides within the solar system. Einstein's equation predicted the universe is in a dynamic state of expansion. In his book *The Science of God*, Dr. Gerald Schroeder stated that Einstein did not like the predictions of his equation that the universe is not static. Einstein introduced a cosmological constant to the equation to "religiously" keep his belief that the universe is eternal, following Plato and the fathers of modern philosophy. Einstein later admitted that introducing the cosmological constant was the biggest blunder of his career. With the Hubble Telescope observation in 1929, Einstein later conceded to the actual prediction of his original equation.

The implication of the big bang and a dynamically expanding universe is a precursor to why many astrophysicists and scientists hold that a creator exists today. I once read that Gerald Schroeder's work contributed to the conversion of Antony Flew, one of the leading atheists in the world at that time, to conclude that God existed before he died.

Some scientists have used the analogy of a balloon to explain the big bang and the expansion of the universe. Think of the universe as an expanding balloon with marks on it; the implication is that as the balloon expands, you will observe every spot on it as moving away from neighboring sites in every direction. Similarly, the universe's galaxies are moving away from the Milky Way. Such receding galaxies were what the Hubble Space Telescope observed. The argument then builds that it logically follows that there must be a time in a finite past where the universe would have been so condensed to a state of infinite density. The conclusion is that the universe began as a single point of an infinitely dense state that expanded to the astronomically large and less dense universe that we know today. Therefore, the universe has a beginning, often called a singularity point. One of the supports of this assertion is the cosmic microwave background radiation. (CMBR)

CMBR is what scientists theorize as the remnants of the heat generated during the earliest history of the universe. At the earliest observable moment of the big bang, the universe began with a burst of energy, resulting in a very hot universe of infinite density. The temperature was initially high, but as the universe began to expand, it cooled as it became less dense. Scientists theorized that CMBR indicates an initial violent outburst of energy in the universe. CMBR has been observed in every direction that scientists have looked as they investigate the universe.

William L. Craig, PhD., used the big bang theory to revisit the Kalam cosmological argument for the beginning and cause of the universe. Dr. Craig argued using three premises of the Kalam cosmological argument. The three premises of his argument are as follows:

1. Whatever begins to exist has a cause.
2. The universe began to exist.
3. Therefore, the universe has a cause.

The argument then goes further to say that whatever caused the universe to come into existence must then transcend all we know scientifically today that began with universe existence: space, time, matter, and energy. The cause of the universe then must be beyond space and matter (immaterial), must be timeless (eternal), and must have an infinite amount of power and energy. This logic then begins to point to what looks like an uncaused, timeless, immaterial entity, with enormous power that transcends and exists before the universe—that looks strikingly like God according to the Bible: "In the beginning, God created" (Genesis 1:1).

Why There Being a God is Plausible—The Universe Is Fine-Tuned for Life

The precision of the laws, forces, and constants of nature has been used to argue why God's existence is highly plausible. Below are details on some of the facts and concepts about the fine-tuning of the universe and the precision of some of the values of the constant of nature. There are four fundamental forces of nature, and they are:

1. gravity,
2. the weak nuclear force,
3. the electromagnetic force, and
4. the strong nuclear force.

These forces are so critical that scientists have used them to explain how objects or particles interact and how certain particles decay. Several universal constants are associated with these laws, like the gravitational constant, speed of light in vacuum, Planck's constant, proton mass, electron mass, the cosmological constant, etc. These constants are crucial for the existence of the laws of nature and physics and, consequently, life's reality. Otherwise, things would never occur in any predictive manner in nature. If any of these laws of physics and forces do not exist, then there could be no life as we know it. The following discusses the precision of the fundamental forces.

1. Gravitational Force Precision: The universal constant precision for the existence of God stems from what is often called the fine-tuning of the universal constants. I will explain my understanding from the works I have read on this. Consider that the possible range of the value of gravitational force is a tape measure having one-inch increments and stretched about fourteen billion light-years (a light-year is the distance that light travels in a year, and the speed of light is about 300000000 m/s). Suppose the tape length represents all the possible locations that the value of the gravitational force of attraction could take in a one-inch (2.54 cm) increment. What was determined is that the gravitational force's magnitude is just at the correct increment in the entire length of the measuring tape. If the value were to move one inch left or right of the measuring tape, life as we know it would cease to exist. Conscious life could never exist if the gravitational force's value were slightly off. That is how fine-tuned the constant of nature is. Therefore it is most likely that someone set the value for it to be that precise. It's like having an alarm clock go off at precisely the same time every day; our experience tells us that it must have been set to do so.

2. Cosmological Constant Precision: Similarly, the cosmological constant that determines the speed of expansion of the universe is so fine-tuned that the universe happened to be expanding at a rate so accurate that that is

the only way we could have material objects formed. Physicists have determined that the cosmological constant's precision is such that we could compare it to traveling several hundreds of miles into space, throwing a dart at a target on the earth, and hitting a bull's eye in an area less than the width of a single atom.

3. Nuclear Forces Precision: The strong nuclear force is also fine-tuned such that it has the proper strength to hold and bind together fundamental particles that form the nucleus of atoms. A slight change in the nuclear force will cause the universe to have hydrogen as the only available element. How is that for the obliteration of chemical life?

A great mind once said that the precision of the universal constants is like trying to find one atom in an entire known universe and you happened to pick that atom on your first try. Looking at such precision, it seems logical that if we compare the existence of our universe to the roll of a dice, the chances that these values will be this precise suggest that it is fine-tuned to give the outcome and not just a product of chance. Therefore, it is almost impossible to escape the conclusion that our universe is designed and set to exist the way it is. That implies that our universe was conceived of by a conscious mind. One of the possible ways some scientists have tried to deflect the unavoidable consequence of the fine-tuning of the universe is the postulate that there are multiple universes. But like I said earlier, this does not soften the ultimate question of how the parallel universes began. How do we falsify the parallel universe theory? No way!

The above reasoning about scientific findings has been used to argue for the existence of a creator. However, a very beautifully written book that discusses these in detail with other scientific findings suggesting there must be a creator is *Case for a Creator* by Lee Strobel.

Creation of Something from Nothing—a Scientific Theory?

It appears that the scientific community has come to a point where some scientists are now open to the possibility that the universe can create itself from nothing. I think this proposition opens new possibilities for a rational conscious creator. Given the state of knowledge in cosmology and quantum physics, it seems that scientists have finally "discovered God" since some scientists are attributing the creative ability to forces of nature.

Dr. Gerald Schroeder, arguing for the existence of God, said that if you discuss with mainline atheists today, they most likely would find it more challenging to disagree with you that science has discovered God. His argument stems from observing the WMAP found on the NASA website: WMAP stands for Wilkinson Microwave Anisotropy Probe. According to NASA, WMAP is a NASA Explorer mission that launched in June 2001 to make fundamental measurements of cosmology—the study of the properties of our universe. WMAP has been stunningly successful, producing our new Standard Model of Cosmology. WMAP's data stream has ended. Full data analysis is now complete.

WMAP published a diagram about the universe's timeline as it expanded from the creation of the universe by the big bang till recent history, spanning about 13.77 billion years. See the picture in figure 2. This diagram essentially summarizes the current state of knowledge about how scientists or cosmologists believe the universe was created till our present time. The left side of the chart is the beginning of the universe, and the right represents our day. In the universe's earliest years, scientists observed events like the initial burst of energy, inflation, and quantum fluctuations. Each vertical line in the diagram is a billion years. The chart shows the period scientists now call the Dark Ages when they believed the first stars formed, billions of years when the planets and the galaxies formed, and a period of accelerated expansion of the universe. When you look at the diagram, the black region Dr. Schroeder asserts is *nothing*. The "tunnel" of the chart is space—which is something. Outside of the funnel shape is nothing.

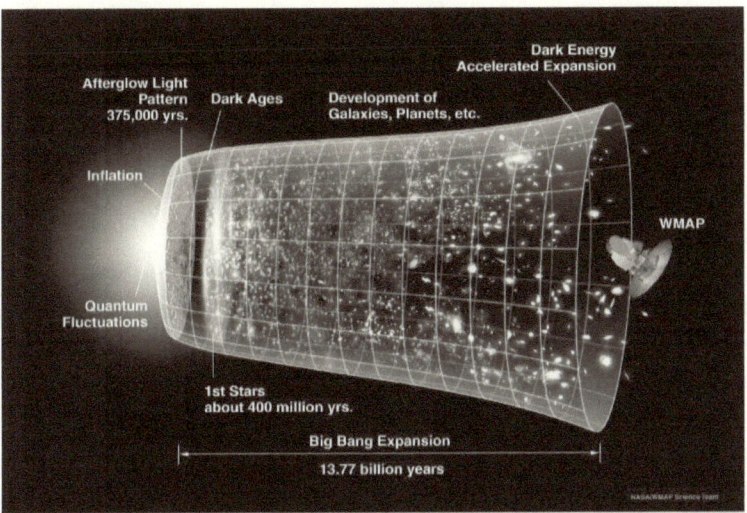

Figure 2: Picture of the representation of the evolution of the universe from the NASA Wilkinson Microwave Anisotropy Probe (WMAP) website

There is a framework developed by Dr. Schroeder in his book "*The Science of God*" that provided one possible way to align the scientific claim to 13.77 Billion years since the creation of the universe with the biblical 6-day creation. According to scientists, what caused the beginning is quantum fluctuations—essentially the creative force. I found the quote below in an article on Space.com, published on June 24, 2021, by Mike Wall, titled "The Big Bang Didn't Need God to Start Universe":

> "Quantum mechanical fluctuations can produce the cosmos," said panelist Seth Shostak, a senior astronomer at the nonprofit Search for Extraterrestrial Intelligence (SETI) Institute. "If you would just, in this room, just twist time and space the right way, you might create an entirely new universe. It's not clear you could get into that universe, but you would create it." He further said, "So it

could be that this universe is merely the science fair project of a kid in another universe," Shostak added. "I don't know how that affects your theological leanings, but it is something to consider."

Essentially, scientists seem to be willing to agree that the universe could have forces that created it, represented by fields whose value fluctuates randomly — quantum fluctuations, appearing as virtual particles created spontaneously.

An American astrophysicist and professor of astronomy at the University of California, Alexei Vladimir "Alex" Filippenko, stressed that such statements are not attacks on the existence of God. In an article in space.com titled "The Big Bang Didn't Need God to Start Universe, Researchers Say", Filippenko said, " Saying the big bang —a massive expansion 13.7 billion years ago that blew space up like a gigantic balloon—could have occurred without God is a far cry from saying that God doesn't exist." He also said, "I don't think you can use science to either prove or disprove the existence of God."

Another exciting quote is in the article published by Bruce Dorminey in *Forbes*, titled *"Cosmic Inflation Was Likely Not A One-Off Event, Says Astronomer"*:

> The cosmic inflation credited with creating the homogeneous universe, which we now enjoy, was likely not a one-off event...these 'whooshes of creation' may be producing multiverses even at this moment.

Edward P. Tryon was an American scientist and a professor emeritus of physics at Hunter College of the City University of New York (CUNY). He was the first physicist to propose that our universe originated as a quantum fluctuation of the vacuum. In an article on Huffpost.com, "Why Isn't Edward P. Tryon A World-famous Physicist?" by Peter Reynosa, it was stated that "Dr. Tryon suggested that 'something could have come from nothing and not break the law of the conservation of energy…that the laws of physics explain how this actually could have taken place.'"

Gerald Schroeder stated in an interview that Edward Tryon published an article in the *Journal of Nature* (*The Journal of Nature* is one of the two leading peer-reviewed journals in America). that the universe allows the creation of something from nothing provided you have the laws of nature

Here, I quote an entire section of an article in *Quanta Magazine* titled "Gravity Creates Something from Nothing" by Natalie Wolchover :

> Particles can display many interesting and surprising phenomena. We can have spontaneous particle creation, entanglement between the states of particles that are far apart, and particles in a superposition of existence in multiple locations. In quantum gravity, space-time itself behaves in novel ways. Instead of the creation of particles, we have the creation of universes…When we consider gravity, we find that the expansion of the universe appears to produce more of this vacuum stuff out of nothing. When space-time is created, it just happens to be in the state that corresponds to the vacuum without any defects…In both cases, there is a kind of stretching of space-time that results in the creation of more of the vacuum substance.

The position of the statement above is like what we quoted Stephen Hawking to have said earlier that gravity, one of the fundamental forces of nature, and quantum fluctuation are said to have the ability to cause the creation of the universe out of nothing.

"The laws and forces of nature are not physical; they act on the physical," says Dr. Schroeder. In essence, if the forces of nature cause the universe to be (i.e., they predate the universe), then they are not physical.

According to Dr. Schroeder, we then have a set of forces with the following attributes:

1. They are not physical
2. They act on the physical
3. They could create the physical from nothing
4. They predate the universe (our understanding of time)

Is It God's Word or the Forces of Nature That Created the Universe?

The question is how much do the attributes of these "creative forces" look like that of the biblical God? See the following scripture to see how similar what the scientist calls the laws or forces of nature are to what the Bible calls the Word of God:

Genesis 1:1–3 (ESV)—"In the beginning, God created the heavens and the earth. The earth was without form and void, and darkness was over the face of the deep. And the Spirit of God was hovering over the face of the waters. And God said, 'Let there be light,' and there was light".

Hebrews 11:3 (KJV)—"Through faith we understand that the worlds were framed by the word of God, so that things which are seen were not made of things which do appear."

Romans 4:16–17 (KJV)—"Therefore it is of faith, that it might be by grace; to the end the promise might be sure to all the seed; not to that only which is of the law, but to that also which is of the faith of Abraham; who is the father of us all. (As it is written, I have made thee a father of many nations,) before him whom he believed, even God, who quickeneth the dead, **and calleth those things which be not as though they were.**"

John 1:1–3 (KJV)—"In the beginning was the Word, and the Word was with God, and the Word was God. The same was in the beginning with God. All things were made by him, and without him was not anything made that was made."

Hebrews 11:3 (ESV) — By faith we understand that the **universe was created by the word of God**, so that what is seen was not made out of things that are visible.

Hebrews 1:3 (TPT)—"The Son is the dazzling radiance of God's splendor, the exact expression of God's true nature—his mirror image! **He holds the universe together and expands it by the mighty power of His spoken word**. He accomplished for us the complete cleansing of sins, and then took his seat on the highest throne at the right hand of the majestic One."

Hebrews 1:8 (TPT)—"**But about His Son, he called him 'God,'** saying, 'Your throne, O God, endures forever and ever and you will rule your kingdom with justice and righteousness.'"

Essentially, one could ask that if scientists are willing to accept that the universe could create itself out of nothing via the forces of nature, is it impossible then to believe that God could have made the universe from nothing by His spoken word? What comes to mind is how we are willing to accept the concept of force as a fact of existence but are willing to question the existence of a conscious rational being and intelligence called God even though we exist as conscious rational beings. I want to bring your attention to some quotes I found while working on my PhD.

Morton Gurtin, in *Configurational Forces as Basic Concepts of Continuum Physics*, argued that forces are a "mathematical construct to make sense of causation." He referred to the work of scientists in the era following the time of Newton and quoted them in his book.

Charles Sanders Peirce, *an American philosopher, mathematician and scientist*, in Collected papers, Harvard University Press, Cambridge stated that:

[Forces are] the great misconception which, developed in the early part of the seventeenth century from the crude idea of cause, and constantly improved upon since, has shown us how to explain all of the changes of motion which body experience, and how to think about physical phenomena; which has given birth to modern science; and which…has played a principal part in directing the course of modern thought…It is, therefore, worth some pain to comprehend it.

Jean-Baptiste le Rond d'Alembert, *a French mathematician, physicist, and philosopher*, spoke of Newtonian forces as **"obscure and metaphysical beings, capable of nothing but spreading darkness over a science clear by itself."**

Pierre Louis Maupertuis, *a French mathematician, biologist, and astronomer who helped popularize Newtonian mechanics*, said **"We speak of forces only to conceal our ignorance"**

Sous-lieutenant Nicolas Léonard Sadi Carnot, *a French mechanical engineer in the French Army, military scientist and physicist, and often described as the "father of thermodynamics*, said **"an obscure metaphysical notion, that of force"**

To the early scientists in the era that follows the time of Newton, the idea of force was not as straightforward as we seem to look at it today. We have come to accept it because it has helped us make sense of the physical world. What if what we call forces is our limited way of understanding how God's word has set the universe to operate and hold together according to the scriptures?

The universe seems to follow precise mathematical form in its operation, and we can understand it through mathematics. Such orderliness of the universe suggests that, just as spoken words only make sense when they have a precise pattern that leads to understanding, God has communicated the universe into being such that the universe makes sense. This sounds consistent with Proverbs 3:19 (NIV)—"By wisdom, the LORD laid the earth's foundations, by understanding he set the heavens in place"—and Proverbs 8:1–3, 22–28 (TPT):

> Can't you hear the voice of Wisdom? From the top of the mountains of influence she speaks into the gateways of the glorious city. At the place where pathways merge, at the entrance of every portal, there she stands, ready to impart understanding, shouting aloud to all who enter, preaching her sermon to those who will listen…In the beginning, I was there, for God possessed me even before he created the universe. From eternity past I was set in place, before the world began. I was anointed from the beginning. Before the oceans depths were poured out, and before there were any glorious fountains overflowing with water, I was there, dancing! Even before one mountain had been sculpted or one hill raised up, I was already there, dancing! When he created the earth, the fields, even the first atom of dust, I was already there. When he hung the tapestry of the heavens and stretched out the horizon of the earth, when the clouds and skies were set in place and the subterranean fountains began to flow strong, I was already there. When he set in place the pillars of the earth and spoke the decrees of the seas, commanding the waves so that they wouldn't overstep their boundaries, I was there, close to the creator's side as his master artist. Daily he was filled with delight in me as I playfully rejoiced before him. I laughed and played, so happy with what he had made, while finding my delight in the children of men.

I will say that gone are the days when it is scientifically more difficult to believe in the existence of God.

The God of the Skeptics

God did not leave the skeptics and agnostics without the telltale signs of His existence. These signs are in His creation. I call the telltale signs the silent preachers. They quietly speak to us as revealed in the book of Psalm 19:1–4:

> The heavens tell about the glory of God. The skies announce what his hands have made. Each new day tells more of the story, and each night reveals more and more about God's power. You cannot hear them say anything. They don't make any sound we can hear. But their message goes throughout the world. Their teaching reaches the ends of the earth. The sun's tent is set up in the heavens.

Now, let us see what the Bible says about the existence of a creator:

> Romans 1:19–20: "For what can be known about God is plain to them, because God has shown it to them. For his invisible attributes, namely, his eternal power and divine nature, have been clearly perceived, ever since the creation of the world, in the things that have been made. So they are without excuse.

My earlier argument using your existence aligns with Romans 1:19. Romans 1:20 now support the rest of the discussions. Supported by Psalm 19:1–4, observation of the universe and created things is how we perceive God. The Bible strongly suggests that God fills nature or creation with obvious telltale signs of His existence so that no one can miss Him—therefore, there can be no excuse. This obviousness of God in nature may explain why the Scripture says that only a fool will say that there is no God in His heart.

So when you see the moon, stars, sun, billions of galaxies, billions of stars within the billions of galaxies, the constellations, neutron stars, black holes, trees, birds, fishes, air, water, ice, snow, and on and on, the existing creations in the universe point to the handiworks of God, the creator. That is the affirmation of the scriptures. If only you knew how big our universe is, you would want to know God intimately. I hope you can conclude like myself that He exists. He is incredible, enormous, immense, infinitely incomprehensible, simply knowable, and significantly and infinitely powerful. The more you know Him, the more you are mesmerized to think that He could be a Father to you—which is the message of the New Covenant that Jesus and all His followers preach as the good news.

Let me summarize the key points for my argument that there is a God:

1. I made an argument based on your existence that God could exist as a conscious being.
2. I argued based on what scientists have observed and have agreed to about how our universe began.
3. I argued based on the precision and fine-tuning of the universe.
4. I argued that God exists by alluding that scientists attribute creation to forces of nature.
5. I argued based on what the Bible says about the handiworks of God pointing to God in creation.

Finally, I want to state that God must exist based on arguments from morality. The idea that we attribute fundamental and objective moral value to humans suggests that there must be a God who instills this value within us. Otherwise, from whom did we get this conscience – a law within us"? Romans 2:14–16 (TPT):

> For when Gentiles, who **do not have the law**, by nature do what the law requires, **they are a law to themselves [moral sense],** even though they do not have the law. They show that the work of the law is written on their

hearts, while **their conscience also bears witness**, and their conflicting thoughts accuse or even excuse.

When you put all these together, I contend that *there is a God.* What do you say?

Chapter Four

Why Rely on the Bible?

A Surer Word

In chapter 2, I took the premise of my argument from the Bible that a good, omnibenevolent, omniscient, omnipotent, omnipresent God exists simultaneously with evil, pain, and suffering. I am writing this chapter to help you, who object to my argument because you think the Bible is unreliable. Hopefully, you will believe and take the Bible as a reliable book for life at the end of this chapter. Consequently, you can find hope in the faithful promises and insight provided in the Bible during life storms.

Why should we believe the Bible? We should believe the Bible is trustworthy because of:

1. The claim of those who wrote it as documentation of the events that they were eyewitnesses of because the Spirit of God moved them
2. The historical credibility of the Bible itself as a reliable piece of an ancient document

I will now discuss why we should rely on the Bible from these two perspectives.

An Ancient Historical Document

Regardless of where you stand on the reliability of the claims of the Bible, one thing you will agree to after thorough research is that the Bible is a collection of historically reliable documents. Most scholars agree that the gospels in the Bible are an attempt to write the biography of Jesus by eyewitnesses who lived in the days of Christ or by men who had direct contact with eyewitnesses. And their goal was to ensure they presented the truth of what happened during the life of Jesus Christ as accurately as they could because they knew the story to be true. Clear evidence of this from scripture is the statement in the first few verses of the book of Luke 1:1–4 (ERV) and Acts 1:1 (TPT):

> Luke 1:1–4 "Most Honorable Theophilus: Many others have tried to give a report of the things that happened among us to complete God's plan. What they have written agrees with what we learned from the people who saw those events from the beginning. They also served God by telling people his message. I studied it all carefully from the beginning. Then I decided to write it down for you in an organized way. I did this so that you can be sure that what you have been taught is true."

> Acts 1:1—"To Theophilus, the lover of God. I write to you again, my dear friend, to give you further details about the life of our Lord Jesus and all the things that he did and taught."

Luke made it clear that the things he wrote to Theophilus both in Luke's gospel and the book of the Acts of the Apostles were reports of what happened after carefully investigating the accuracy and integrity of the claims about the life and ministry of Jesus. It is worth noting that Jesus quoted a lot from the Hebrew Bible (Moses, Abraham, the law, Psalms, and the prophets). His early apostles did the same. Luke writes here as a trained historian who has carefully investigated and presented an orderly account of Jesus's life. Some scholars have noted that the people in the New Testament era did value eyewitness testimony, which would explain why Luke sought out eyewitness accounts. Peter also strengthened what Luke said about Christ by saying that he was an eyewitness himself in 2 Peter 1:18–21 (TPT):

> **And we ourselves heard that voice resound from the heavens while we were with him on the holy mountain.** And so we have been given the prophetic word—the written message of the prophets, made more reliable and fully validated by the confirming voice of God on the Mount of Transfiguration. And you will continue to do well if you stay focused on it. For this prophetic message is like a piercing light shining in a gloomy place until the dawning of a new day, when the Morning Star rises in your hearts. You must understand this at the outset: Interpretation of scriptural prophecy requires the Holy Spirit, for it does not originate from someone's own imagination. No true prophecy comes from human initiative but is inspired by the moving of the Holy Spirit upon those who spoke the message that came from God.

Similarly, John the Beloved also said that he spoke of what he had seen and handled as an eyewitness in 1 John 1:1–3 (TPT):

> **We saw him with our very own eyes.** We gazed upon him and heard him speak. Our hands actually touched him, the one who was from the beginning, the Living Expression of God. This Life-Giver was made visible and we have seen him. We testify to this truth: the eternal Life-Giver lived face-to-face with the Father and has now dawned upon us. So we proclaim to you what we have seen and heard about this Life-Giver so that we may share and enjoy this life together. For truly our fellowship is with the Father and with His Son, Jesus, the Anointed One.

So we have at least three eyewitness testimonies of the reliability of the gospels and the epistles; this is consistent with the rule of eyewitness account reliability as written in 2 Corinthians 13:1 (TPT): "This will be my third trip to you. And I will make sure that **by the testimony of two or three witnesses every matter will be confirmed.**" This echoes Deuteronomy 19:5:

> A single witness shall not suffice against a person for any crime or for any wrong in connection with any offense that he has committed. **Only on the evidence of two witnesses or of three witnesses shall a charge be established.**

Although scholarly opinion might defer on the details, the gospel account is seen as the writings of eyewitness accounts by the Ante-Nicene Fathers. Some of the Ante-Nicene Fathers of the church were the disciples of the direct apostles of Jesus Christ. According to Jerome (one of the post-Nicene fathers, who translated the Greek New Testament into the Latin Vulgate), Polycarp, one of the Ante-Nicene Fathers and a Christian bishop of Smyrna was a direct disciple of John the Beloved.

One of the arguments most skeptics put against the reliability of the New Testament gospel accounts is their "seeming" contradictions. A skeptic once challenged me about this some time ago while I was sharing the gospel on a platform. I remember going back to the gospels, mainly related to the account of Jesus's death and resurrection. At first look, there are appearances of contradictions in the gospel accounts. However, after a couple of thoughts and research, it became apparent that what appeared to be a contradiction is clear evidence supporting the reliability of the gospel account. The reason is that if all gospel accounts (which, according to scholars, were eyewitness accounts) all agree on the details, it would be easy to accuse the authors of conspiracy. However, an accurate eyewitness account should have minor differences in the information presented by different eyewitnesses to help put the pieces of what happened together. While I was researching this seeming contradiction, I found the work of American author J. Warner Wallace titled *Cold-Case Christianity: A Homicide Detective Investigates the Claims of the Gospels.* You might read that book to help you make sense of how those seeming contradictions help to support the reliability of the accounts in the gospel.

I remember going back and creating a document to see if I could align the four gospels into a single story of the resurrection account. I found out that there are many ways that I could do that convincingly. I did this with my wife. An example that I put together with my wife is detailed in the next section.

Harmonizing the Four Gospels: Jesus's Resurrection Accounts

In this section, I will present an example of a narrative that shows that there is no contradiction in the gospel accounts. The narrative below is the harmonization of the resurrection account from Matthew 28:1–17, Mark 16:1–8, Luke 24:1–11, and John 20:1–18.

> Now after the Sabbath, when the Sabbath was past, on the first day of the week—as the first day of the week began to dawn. Very early in the morning, early while it was still dark, they (women of Galilee—Luke 23:55–56— which includes May Magdalene, Mary the mother of James, and Salome (see Matthew, Mark, John)), and certain other women with them, went to the tomb. They came to see the tomb when the sun had risen bringing the spices which they had prepared that they might come and anoint Him.
>
> And behold, there was (there had been (AMP version)) a great earthquake; for an angel of the Lord descended from heaven and came and rolled back the

stone from the door and sat on it. His countenance was like lightning, and his clothing as white as snow. And the guards shook for fear of him and became like dead men. And they (Mary Magdalene, Mary the mother of James, and Salome) said among themselves, "Who will roll away the stone from the door of the tomb for us?" But when they looked up they (the women of Galilee including Mary Magdalene, Mary the mother of James, Salome, and the other women—Luke 24:1) saw and found the stone had been rolled away and had been taken away from the tomb for it was very large.

Then they (the women of Galilee and the other women—Luke 24:1) went in and did not find the body of the Lord Jesus. And entering the tomb, they [Mary Magdalene, Mary the mother of James, and Salome] saw a young man clothed in a long white robe sitting on the right side; and they were alarmed. But the angel (young man) answered and said to them (Mary Magdalene and the other Mary and Salome), "Do not be afraid. Do not be alarmed for I know that you seek Jesus of Nazareth, who was crucified. He is not here; for, He is risen! as He said. Come, see the place where the Lord lay, where they laid Him. And go quickly and tell His disciples that He is risen from the dead, and indeed He is going before you into Galilee; there you will see Him. Behold, I have told you."

So they (Mary Magdalene, Mary the mother of James, and Salome) went out quickly from the tomb and fled from the tomb with fear and great joy, for they trembled and were amazed. And they said nothing to anyone, for they were afraid, and ran to bring His disciples word.

Then she (Mary Magdalene) ran and came to Simon Peter, and to the other disciple, whom Jesus loved, and said to them, "They have taken away the Lord out of the tomb, and we do not know where they have laid Him."

Now while they were going (Mary Magdalene and Mary the mother of James), behold, some of the guard came into the city and reported to the chief priests all the things that had happened. When they had assembled with the elders and consulted together, they gave a large sum of money to the soldiers, saying, "Tell them, 'His disciples came at night and stole Him away while we slept.' And if this comes to the governor's ears, we will appease him and make you secure." So they took the money and did as they were instructed, and this saying is commonly reported among the Jews until this day.

And it happened, as they (the rest of the women in Luke 24:1, excluding Mary Magdalene, Mary the mother of James, and Salome, who had left at the instruction of the young man) were greatly perplexed about this, that behold, two men stood by them in shining garments. Then, as they were afraid and bowed their faces to the earth, they said to them, "Why do you seek the living among the dead? He is not here, but is risen! Remember how He spoke to you when He was still in Galilee, saying, 'The Son of Man must be delivered into the hands of sinful men, and be crucified, and the third day rise again.'" And they remembered His words.

Then they returned from the tomb and told all these things to the eleven and to all the rest. It was Mary Magdalene, Joanna, Mary the mother of James, and the other women with them, who told these things to the apostles. And their words seemed to them like idle tales, and they did not believe them.

But Peter arose and ran to the tomb; and stooping down, he saw the linen cloths lying by themselves; and he departed, marveling to himself at what had happened. Peter therefore went out, and the other disciple, and were going to the tomb. So they both ran together, and the other disciple outran Peter and came to the tomb first. And he, stooping down and looking in, saw the linen cloths lying there; yet he did not go in. Then Simon Peter came, following him, and went into the tomb; and he saw the linen cloths lying there, and the handkerchief that had been around His head, not lying with the linen cloths, but folded together in a place by itself. Then the other disciple, who came to the tomb first, went in also; and he saw and believed. For as yet they did not know the scripture, that He must rise again from the dead.

Then the disciples went away again to their own homes. But Mary stood outside by the tomb weeping, and as she wept she stooped down and looked into the tomb. And she saw two angels in white sitting, one at the head and the other at the feet, where the body of Jesus had lain. Then they said to her, "Woman, why are you weeping?" She said to them, "Because they have taken away my Lord, and I do not know where they have laid Him." Now when she had said this, she turned around and saw Jesus standing there, and did not know that it was Jesus. Jesus said to her, "Woman, why are you weeping? Whom are you seeking?" She, supposing Him to be the gardener, said to Him, "Sir, if You have carried Him away, tell me where You have laid Him, and I will take Him away." Jesus said to her, "Mary!" She turned and said to Him, "Rabboni!" (which is to say, Teacher). Jesus said to her, "Do not cling to Me, for I have not yet ascended to My Father; but go to My brethren and say to them, 'I am ascending to My Father and your Father, and to My God and your God.'"

Mary Magdalene came and told the disciples that she had seen the Lord, and that He had spoken these things to her. (The disciples got to know He was Alive as summarized below)

Now when He (Jesus) rose early on the first day of the week, He appeared first to Mary Magdalene (as described above), out of whom He had cast seven demons. She went and told those (the rest according to Luke 24:9) who had been with Him (Jesus) as they mourned and wept. And when they heard that He was alive and had been seen by her, they did not believe. And as they went to tell His disciples, behold, Jesus met them, saying, "Rejoice!" So they came and held Him by the feet and worshiped Him. Then Jesus said to them, "Do not be afraid. Go and tell My brethren to go to Galilee, and there they will see Me."

You could do the same exercise and find another way to align the four-resurrection account into a single story. I argue that since we were not there as eyewitnesses, we cannot know for sure that each of our sequences of the account is how the event unfolded. However, we would agree that we could put the four gospel accounts into one story, which I have demonstrated above.

Like the seeming contradiction that called for aligning the four-gospel account of Jesus's resurrection above, some other challenge that skeptics put forward against the gospel is a claim to apparent contradictions in the report of the gospels' accounts of similar stories. We can efficiently resolve these seeming difficulties with the idea that two eyewitnesses of an event do not necessarily give the same report. Each eyewitness reports aspects of the events as they observe them, as they prefer to share it based on the part of the event that interests them and their intended audience. Such differences in accounts in no way diminishes the authority or inerrancy of scripture.

The Bible was not supposed to be nor did it claim to be a book dropped down from the sky by some magic. The Bible is a book of divine inspiration interwoven with the experience of human life through history to deliver God's perspective on existence. I believe the Bible reveals God Himself, shows God's redemptive work on humanity, and demonstrates how God wants us to have a loving and yet covenant relationship with Him to make us His sons and daughters for all eternity. So divinity and humanity coexist in the Bible just as divinity and humanity coexist in the central person in the Bible—Jesus Christ. Yet both the Bible and Jesus are perfect without error when we correctly understand them.

Accuracy and Authenticity of the Bible

Most scholars agree with the following facts that help support the claim that the Bible is a reliable historical document:

1. Jesus's public ministry took place between AD 27–AD 30.
2. Jesus died between AD 30 and AD 33.
3. The gospel of Mark was written first (which is most likely Mark's account of Peter's eyewitness account, and it was written between AD 60 and AD 75.
4. The Gospel of Matthew and Luke were written sometime between AD 60 and AD 90.
5. The Gospel of John was written between AD 70 and AD 100.

Based on these timelines, it is evident that eyewitnesses wrote the gospel accounts while other eyewitnesses were still alive and around. So we have a historical document written most likely by eyewitnesses or those who interviewed eyewitnesses while other eyewitnesses were still alive. If these accounts were false, they would have been contested by other eyewitnesses who were still alive. On the contrary, other historians like Josephus and Tacitus corroborated the reports and claims of the gospel about Jesus. For example, in Josephus's history of the Jewish book in AD 93, *Antiquities of the Jews*, there is a generally agreed upon quotation about Jesus:

> Now there was about this time Jesus, a wise man, if it be lawful to call him a man; for he was a doer of wonderful works, a teacher of such men as receive the truth with pleasure. He drew over to him both many of the Jews and many of the Gentiles. He was [the] Christ. And when Pilate, at the suggestion of the principal men amongst us, had condemned him to the cross, those that loved him at the first did not forsake him; for he appeared to them alive again the third day; as the divine prophets had foretold these and ten thousand other wonderful things

concerning him. And the tribe of Christians, so named from him, are not extinct at this day. (Josephus, Book XVIII, chapter 3)

One of the things I found while I was researching to write this chapter is the strength of the oral tradition during the biblical period. It is not just one person telling the story; an entire community is there to challenge, correct, and ensure the accuracy of the story being told, particularly of something considered sacred. It is like the peer-review process that we have in the academic community today regarding how peers ensure the accuracy of the transfer of knowledge. This community is the community of disciples.

The earliest manuscript of the gospel written on papyrus and animal skin sheets dates back as one of the oldest existing manuscripts of ancient writings, which include:

1. Codex Sinaiticus (AD 330 and AD 350) contains all the New Testament scriptures and some of the old
2. Codex Vaticanus, a nearly complete Greek copy of the entire Bible, dates about the same era as Codex Sinaiticus (AD 300–325).

There are no original manuscripts of the New Testaments but copies. Since these were copies, skeptics believe that the New Testament accounts are unreliable. However, some scholars have noted that the manuscript of the New Testaments has better attestation than any ancient document. The New Testament Bible has over five thousand Greek manuscripts.

Another support for the New Testament scriptures is the quotation from the early fathers of the church. Scholars agreed that the early church fathers quoted the New Testaments so much that we could reconstruct the entire New Testament using quotations from the church fathers.

Some scholars have noted that the Gnostic Gospels are different from the four gospels (written in the first century

AD). The Gnostic Gospels were written in the second century AD. The Gnostic Gospels presented a different kind of Jesus compared to the four gospels and were not written as eyewitness accounts or testimony of eyewitness accounts. Therefore, they are less reliable, if not altogether unreliable. It has been suggested that the canonization of the Bible is not about different gospel accounts competing for survival, where only the ones that survived were the ones that made it to the scriptures. The prevalent argument is that the canonized four gospels are the most accurate account. Their dates are much closer to the time when Jesus lived as a first-century Jew, not a second-century Roman or Greek person as the Gnostic Gospels portray him.

The Bible Is the Word of God: It Is Reliable!

The Bible is the Word of God. The authors of the Bible and Christians of all ages believe the Bible is the Word of God. If we see the Bible as the Word of God, then we are more likely to put our trust in it because God cannot lie: "So that by two unchangeable things, **in which it is impossible for God to lie**, we who have fled for refuge might have strong encouragement to hold fast to the hope set before us" (Hebrews 6:18 ESV).

Therefore, if the Bible is the Word of God, then it must be speaking the truth on all matters that it addresses. The rest of this section provides some positive evidence that supports the Bible as the Word of God. In his book *Standing on the Rock: Upholding Biblical Authority in a Secular Age*, James Montgomery Boice gives some lines of evidence that the Bible is the Word of God. Some of the lines of argument that support the claim that the Bible is the Word of God include the following:

The Teaching of Christ and His View of the Bible

Jesus Christ is the central theme of the Bible and, if one can take it, of history. Archaeological works have confirmed His history. And the Bible speaks clearly about Jesus and reveals who Jesus is. Beyond the fact that the Bible is a reliable historical document, Jesus quotes a lot from the scriptures in His teachings. Jesus took the scriptures as the Word of God. The attitude of Jesus to the scriptures, more than anything else, supports the fact the Bible is the Word of God. Examples of instances when Jesus quoted the Bible (the Hebrew Bible) as the Word of God include:

1. Temptation by the Devil: Jesus quoted from Deuteronomy 8:3, 6:13, and 6:16 in Matthew 4 and Luke 4 during His temptation by the Devil. He saw the Bible as a written text forever established as a guiding truth for life. For Jesus, what is written in the scriptures is a statement of fact about existence.
2. Reality of resurrection and heavenly marriage status: In Matthew 22:23–33 and Luke 20:27–40, Jesus Christ used scriptures from Exodus 3:6 to respond to the Sadducees' question about the resurrection's reality and used the same instance to teach that marriage is only earthly.
3. Jesus supported and defended His life and actions with scriptures: Jesus defended His cleansing of the temple with the scriptures in Mark 11:15–17. He so believed in the finality of scriptures and that the scriptures could not be broken (John 10:35, Matthew 5:18) that He submitted to the cruel cross of the scripture as recorded in Matthew 26:53–54. It was clear to Jesus that His life was fulfilling the scriptures that He often quoted from the scriptures to support significant events in His life. In Luke 4:18–19, He quoted Isaiah 61:1–2 when He began His ministry. Jesus defended His authority by alluding to the authority of scriptures when talking to the Jewish rulers in John 5:39, 45–47. At the end of Jesus's human life on the cross, He quoted Psalm 22:1 (see Matthew 27:46). Even after His resurrection, Jesus demonstrated that He took the scriptures as the Word of God as written in Luke 24: 25–27:

And he said to them, "O foolish ones, and slow of heart to believe all that the prophets have spoken! Was it not necessary that the Christ should suffer these things and enter into his glory?" And beginning with Moses and all the Prophets, he interpreted to them in all the scriptures the things concerning himself.

In Matthew 26:26–27, Jesus quoted from Exodus 24:8 to speak about the shedding of His blood as a sign of God's covenant.

Jesus claims the authority of scripture as the Word of God. If Jesus claimed to have all authority in heaven and Earth and He quoted scriptures as authoritative, He affirms the authority of the scriptures. Jesus also sent His disciples to go and do likewise (Matthew 28:19–20). So with the authority of Jesus, the disciples He commanded to teach wrote the New Covenant books. These twenty-seven New Testament scriptures are the books written by or connected to some who interacted with His apostles and have apostolic authority or backing. Essentially, the scriptures are authoritative and are the Word of God because Jesus has all authority. He saw the scripture as authoritative and commanded His apostles, who wrote the New Testament, to teach from scriptures.

The Accuracy of Prophecy of the Old Testament

The Bible is a prophetic book. Therefore, just like human prophets spoke the Word of God through their human vessels and their humanity with their spirits being subject to them, the Bible also speaks the Word of God locked within the letter of the history and style of writing. The Word of God comes out of the pages of the scripture when we turn to the Lord Jesus (2 Corinthians 3 and John 5:39–40). Two prophecies of the Bible that came to pass and supported the claim of scriptures as the Word of God were messianic prophecies and prophecy about Israel.

Jesus fulfilled messianic prophecies: The Messiah prophecy predicted in the Old Testament was matched perfectly by Jesus against all mathematical odds. The fulfillment was so accurate that it would look like the prophecies were written after the fact. *Strong's Expanded Exhaustive Concordance* of the Bible lists forty-four prophecies of the Messiah that Jesus fulfilled in order of fulfillment. In each case, the Old Testament text is the prophecy and the New Testament texts are the fulfillment. They are as follows:

The woman's seed—Genesis 3:15, Galatians 4:4
Descendant of Abraham—Genesis 12:3, Matthew 1:1
Descendant of Isaac—Genesis. 17:19, Luke 3:34
Descendant of Jacob—Numbers 24:17, Matthew 1:2
From the Tribe of Judah—Genesis 49:10, Luke 3:33
Heir to David's Throne —Isaiah 9:7, Luke 1:32, 33
Anointed and Eternal—Psalm 45:6,7; 102:25–27,
Hebrews 1:8–12
Born in Bethlehem—Micah 5:2, Luke 2:4,5,7
The Time for His Birth—Daniel 9:25, Luke 2:1–2
To be Born of a Virgin—Isaiah 7:14, Luke 1:26–31
Slaughter of Children to Kill Him—Jeremiah 3:15,
Matthew 2: 16–18
Flight to Egypt—Hosea 11:1, Matthew 2:14, 15
Way Prepared for Him—Isaiah 40:3–5, Luke 3:3–6
Preceded by a Forerunner—Malachi 3:1, Luke 7:24, 27
Preceded by Elijah—Mal 4:5–6; Matthew 11:13–14
Declared the Son of God—Psalm 2:7, Matthew 3:17
He Will Have a Galilean Ministry—Isaiah 9:1–2,
Matthew 4:13–16
He Will Speak in Parables—Psalm 78:2–4, Matthew
13:34–35
He Will Be a Prophet—Deuteronomy 18:5, Acts 3:20, 22
He Will Bind Up the Brokenhearted—Isaiah 61:1–2,
Luke 4:18–19
The Jews Will Reject Him—Isaiah 53:3, John 1:11, Luke
23:18

He Will Be a Priest after the Order of Melchizedek—
Psalm 110:4, Hebrews. 5:5–6

His Triumphal Entry to Jerusalem—Zechariah 9:9, Mark
11:7, 9, 11

He Will Be Adored by Infants Ps 8:2, Matthew 21:15, 16

Many Will Not Believe Him—Isaiah 53:1, John
12:37, 38

He Will Be Betrayed by a Close Friend—Psalm 41:9,
Luke 22:47, 48

Judas Will Betray Him for Thirty Pieces of Silver—
Zechariah 11:12, Matthew. 26:14, 15

He Will Be Accused by False Witnesses—Psalm
35:11, Mark 14:57–58

He Will Be Silent to Accusations—Isaiah 53:7, Mark
15:4–5

He Will Be Spat On and Struck—Isaiah 50:6,
Matthew 26:27

He Will Be Hated Without Reason—Psalm 35:19,
John 15:24–25

He Will Be a Vicarious Sacrifice—Isaiah 53:5,
Romans 5:6, 8

He Will Be Crucified with Transgressors—Isaiah
53:12, Mark 15:27, 28

His Hands and Feet will be Pierced Through—
Zechariah. 12:10, John 20:27

He Will Be Sneered and Mocked—Psalm 22:7, 8,
Luke 23:35

He Will Experience Reproach—Psalm 69:9, Romans
15:3

He Will Pray for His Enemies—Psalm 109:4, Luke
23:34

Soldiers Gambled for His Clothes—Psalm 22:17, 18,
Matthew 27:35, 36

He Will Be Forsaken by God—Psalm 22:1, Matthew
27:46

None of His Bones Will Be Broken—Psalm 34:20,
John 19:32, 33, 36

His Side Will Be Pierced—Zechariah 12:10, John 19:34

He Will Be Buried with the Rich—Isaiah 53:9,
Matthew 27:57–60
He Would Resurrect from the Dead—Psalm16:10,
49:15, Mark 16:6, 7, 1 Corinthians 15:4
He Will Ascend to God's Right Hand—Psalm 68:18,
110:1–3, Mark 16:19, Ephesians 4:8

In 1963, Peter Stoner, a science professor at Westmont College in Santa Barbara, California, did extensive research on the mathematical probabilities (odds) of various numbers of Old Testament prophecies about the Messiah applying to Jesus of Nazareth (*Science Speaks: Scientific Proof of the Accuracy of Prophecy and the Bible*, pg. 101–109). He estimated that it is mathematically impossible that one man could fulfill all these messianic prophecies of the Old Testament. And Jesus fulfilled all of them. These odds support the claim that Jesus must be the Messiah and support the reliability of the Bible.

Prophecy About Israel

The reinstatement of Israel as a nation after centuries of Jews being scattered among the nation is a powerful argument for the reliability of the Bible as the Word of God. In 1948, Israel came back as a nation, fulfilling prophecies by Ezekiel and Isaiah:

> Thus said the Lord God: You, O mountains of Israel, shall yield your produce and bear your fruit for My people Israel, for their return is near. For I will care for you: I will turn to you, and you shall be tilled and sown. I will settle a large population on you, the whole House of Israel; the towns shall be resettled, and the ruined sites rebuilt. I will multiply men and beasts upon you, and they shall increase and be fertile, and I will resettle you as you were formerly and will make you more prosperous than you were at first. And you shall know that I am the Lord. I will lead…My people Israel to you, and they shall

possess you. You shall be their heritage, and you shall not again cause them to be bereaved. (Ezekiel 36:8–12)

Who hath heard such a thing? who hath seen such things? Shall a land be born in one day? Shall a nation be brought forth at once? For as soon as Zion travailed, she brought forth her children. (Isaiah 66:8)

Authority and Inerrancy of Scripture

Biblical inerrancy is the belief that the Bible "is without error or fault in all its teaching", according to Geisler, NL., and Roach, B., in the book *Defending Inerrancy: Affirming the Accuracy of Scripture for a New Generation* or at least that "Scripture in the original manuscripts does not affirm anything contrary to fact." according to Grudem, Wayne A. in the book *Systematic theology: an introduction to biblical doctrine.*

The Bible is a book where God spoke infallibly but through the history of fallible human beings because a transcendent God who exists outside of space, time, matter, and energy wanted to reveal Himself to, have a relationship with, and fulfill His eternal plans with humans. Humans live in space and time, with limited energy, and are mortal, so God decided to reveal Himself, which He does through His spoken word. God decided to have His spoken word immortalized in written texts through the history of fallible human beings so that His words are relatable to humans and yet transcend humanity. The Word of God, therefore, bears the marks of both divinity and humanity and this is consistent with the ultimate revelation of scriptures, which is the person of Jesus Christ, who is 100 percent God and 100 percent man and yet has none of the shortcomings and missing the mark that humans have. In contrast, He lived in space and time in history. Can you see the connection between the authenticity and inerrancy of the written scriptures and the Incarnation of God in the person of Jesus Christ? If Jesus was 100 percent God and 100 percent man and He knew no sin, thereby perfect, then the Bible could also be the Word of God that was written through the human vessel and yet not be fallible.

One of the reasons to take the Bible as the Word of God is that it contains the Ten Commandments. The origin of the Old Testament was a tablet with texts written by the very finger of God after God had spoken to Moses. God most likely used the combination of His spoken word and written word to reveal that He intended that His spoken word would be encapsulated in the written texts. God's Word is how He expresses and reveals Himself, the full revelation of His Word culminating in the person of Jesus Christ. So it is consistent with how God has operated in history to believe that the written text and the coordination of how they all came to tell a single story is an act of God Himself.

In Exodus 19 and 20, as God spoke in thunder and fire and wrote the scripture with His finger, making His writing on the table of stone bear His authority, so do the holy scriptures, written as a textualization of God's Word to prophets, bear the authority of the God who spoke. Hence, the scriptures can be taken as the absolute authority for life and godliness if we can establish that:

1. The event on Sinai, when the Ten Commandments were written, have historical credibility
2. Prophets existed, and they spoke words that came to pass as they predicted under the claim that the omniscient and omnipotent God said it would happen
3. Jesus Christ Himself existed and could be proven to have used the writing of the prophets as authority for life and godliness, and He treated the scriptures as having final authority
4. We can prove that Jesus taught from Old Testament scriptures to His apostles.
5. Jesus asked the apostles to write scriptures after He resurrected and as the Holy Spirit (the Spirit of God—who

was also called the finger of God) is now on them and indwells them

6. The Bible made claims of the divine inspiration of itself.

Claim to Inspiration of the Bible Within Itself

The Bible speaks about itself. The men who wrote the Bible claimed that it was inspired by God: "For **no prophecy was ever produced by the will of** man, **but men spoke from God as the Holy Spirit carried them along.**" (2 Peter 1:21 ESV)

> Peter:
> For we did not follow cleverly devised myths when we made known to you the power and coming of our Lord Jesus Christ, but we were eyewitnesses of his majesty. For when he received honor and glory from God the Father, and the voice was borne to him by the Majestic Glory, "This is my beloved Son, with whom I am well pleased," we ourselves heard this very voice borne from heaven, for we were with him on the holy mountain.
> And we have the prophetic word more fully confirmed, to which you will do well to pay attention as to a lamp shining in a dark place, until the day dawns and the morning star rises in your hearts, knowing this first of all, that no prophecy of scripture comes from someone's own interpretation. **For no prophecy was ever produced by the will of man, but men spoke from God as they were carried along by the Holy Spirit.** (2 Peter 1:16–21)

> Paul:
> **All scripture is given by inspiration of God,** and is profitable for doctrine, for reproof, for correction, for instruction in righteousness: That the man of God may

be perfect, thoroughly furnished unto all good works (2 Timothy 3: 16–17).

But, as it is written, "What no eye has seen, nor ear heard, nor the heart of man imagined, what God has prepared for those who love him" These things God has revealed to us through the Spirit. For the Spirit searches everything, even the depths of God. For who knows a person's thoughts except the spirit of that person, which is in him? So also no one comprehends the thoughts of God except the Spirit of God. Now we have received not the spirit of the world, but the Spirit who is from God, that we might understand the things freely given us by God. **And we impart this in words not taught by human wisdom but taught by the Spirit, interpreting spiritual truths to those who are spiritual** (1 Corinthians 2:9–13).

John:

That which was from the beginning, which we have heard, which we have seen with our eyes, which we looked upon and have touched with our hands, concerning the word of life—the life was made manifest, and we have seen it, and testify to it and proclaim to you the eternal life, which was with the Father and was made manifest to us—that which we have seen and heard we proclaim also to you, so that you too may have fellowship with us; and indeed our fellowship is with the Father and with His Son Jesus Christ. And we are writing these things so that our joy may be complete. This is the message we have heard from him and proclaim to you, that God is light, and in him is no darkness at all (1 John 1:1–5).

The Author of the book of Hebrews:

Long ago, at many times and in many ways, God spoke to our fathers by the prophets, but in these last days he has spoken to us by His Son, whom he appointed the heir of all things, through whom also he created the world. (Hebrews 1:1–2)

The Preservation of the Bible

About forty different authors wrote the Bible in about three main languages across three continents and in the space of about fifteen hundred years. These authors spoke about a corroborative and consistent story of God's love and covenant with humanity and a purpose He would fulfill at the end of time. The Bible has been preserved through history and translated into hundreds of languages. The scriptures have stood the test of time despite a history of attacks, burning of scriptures, drowning of scriptures, years of criticism, etc. The preservation of scripture supported the word of Jesus when He said in Matthew 5:18 and Matthew 24:35, "For indeed, I say to you, until heaven and earth pass away, not an iota, not a dot, will pass from the law until all is accomplished" and "Heaven and Earth will pass away, but my words will not pass away."

Transformation of Men and Women—the Bible Works

One of the most robust supports of the Bible as the Word of God is the countless number of lives that have been changed from the earliest history of the Jews up till the current secular society. Testimonies abound in literature and churches all over the world. Lives of men and women have been transformed; they have made an impact, demonstrated love, joy, peace, and fulfillment, which they attributed to the transforming power of the Bible. The worst of sinners have become the most vigorous missionaries after encountering the Word of God in the Bible. I am also a testament to the truth of the scripture. God spoke to my wife and I from Isaiah 43:1–2 a day before our daughter was born—my daughter whose life prepared me to write this book:

But now thus says the LORD, he who created you, O Jacob, he who formed you, O Israel: "Fear not, for I have redeemed you; I have called you by name, you are mine. When you pass through the waters, I will be with you; and through the rivers, they shall not overwhelm you; when you walk through fire you shall not be burned, and the flame shall not consume you.

We have passed through water, and we have not been overwhelmed, and we have walked through the fire, and we were not burned. There is another in the fire standing next to us whose appearance is like that of the Son of God—He was watching His word to bring it to pass. Through the fire and the waters, our lives have changed. We have inspired many, and this book is another proof that the word God is transforming lives because His words will transform you on the pages of this book.

In addition, we have heard of stories and have seen healings and miracles and supernatural work of God from the days of the Ante-Nicene Fathers till contemporary times. We have witnessed devils cast out, the blind have received sight, the lame have walked, incurable diseases have been healed, the barren have given birth, the dead have been raised to life, and lost and wasted lives have been saved and restored—all of these through the name of Jesus and by faith in the Word of God as written in the Bible. I daresay that despite the mystery, the Bible works, and God works wonders. Hallelujah!

God's word and God are intricately connected, so the purpose of scripture then will be accomplished when it reveals God to us and drives us to God Himself in the person of His Word—Jesus Christ (John 5:39–40). With all the information, evidence, and support for the Bible as an accurate, inerrant, and authoritative Word of God, we have a surer word to base the premise of the theodicy argument and framework in this book. Jesus said, "**No one is good except God ALONE.**"

SECTION 2

ORIGIN OF EVIL & GOD'S ETERNAL PURPOSE

Why Rely on the Bible?

Chapter Five

Perpetration, Perpetuation, and Principle of Evil

The Fall of Lucifer and Man—the Mystery of Iniquity

The focus of this chapter will be on the perpetration and the perpetuation of evil. In Chapters 1 and 2, I mentioned that evil was only logically possible but could not have been perpetrated until the creation of a conscious entity. The self-awareness of created being is the potential for the perpetration of evil, while selfish desire is the driving force for evil. In the same way, godly desire is the driving force for the perpetration and perpetuation of good. James 4:1–2 (TPT) supports this concept:

> What is the cause of your conflicts and quarrels with each other? Doesn't the battle begin inside of you as you fight to have your own way and fulfill your **own desires**? You jealously want what others have so you begin to see yourself as better than others. You scheme with envy and harm others to **selfishly obtain what you crave**—that's why you quarrel and fight. And all the time you don't obtain what you want because you won't ask God for it!

Also, look at James 1:13-18(ESV):

> Let no one say when he is tempted, "I am being tempted by God," for **God cannot be tempted with evil, and he himself tempts no one. But each person is**

tempted when he is lured and enticed by his own desire. Then **desire** when it has conceived gives birth to sin, and sin when it is fully grown brings forth death…

Another excellent scripture about the source of evil is Mark 7:21–23(TPT):

> Evil originates from inside a person. Coming out of a human heart are evil schemes, sexual immorality, theft, murder, adultery, greed, wickedness, treachery, debauchery, jealousy, slander, arrogance, and recklessness. All these corrupt things emerge from within and constantly pollute a person.

The Origin of Evilness

The big question then is "Who is the first conscious being God created that became selfish in his desire and therefore perpetrated the first act of evil?" The answer to that fundamental question is that Lucifer (the original Hebrew word means "shining one," "light-bearer," "the morning star") was the first conscious being who developed a selfish desire (iniquity) and committed the first treason and evil. Lucifer became Satan, or the Devil (which I illustrate as **d**oer of **evil**). So every evil perpetrated or perpetuated in creation traces back to Lucifer. He either does it actively or passively through the "virus of iniquity" that he has put in the system of man at the fall of Adam and Eve.

The fall of Lucifer subjected creation to bondage. After the fall of Lucifer and Man, "the whole world lies in the power of the evil one" (1 John 5:19b ESV). Those who are *not* under his power are the children of God: "We know that we are from God" (1 John 5:19a NLT). Therefore, we see evil today because creation is under the power of the evil one and in bondage as a captive to the Devil. And the same verse, we see that the solution is the manifestation of the children (sons) of God

In the rest of this chapter, I will be discussing the fall of Lucifer, other angels, and humans as the three conscious creations of God among whom there is the **selfish desire** that has leads to the perpetration and perpetuation of evil. Based on the testimony of scriptures, there are two *main* categories of conscious beings that God created in His plan for creation. Psalm 8:1–9 (ESV) gives us who these conscious beings are:

> O LORD, our Lord, how majestic is your name in all the earth! You have set your glory above the heavens. Out of the mouth of babies and infants, you have established strength because of your foes, to still the enemy and the avenger. When I look at your heavens, the work of your fingers, the moon and the stars, which you have set in place, what is man that you are mindful of him, and the son of man that you care for him? Yet you have made him a little lower than the heavenly beings and crowned him with glory and honor. You have given him dominion over the works of your hands; you have put all things under his feet, all sheep and oxen, and also the beasts of the field, the birds of the heavens, and the fish of the sea, whatever passes along the paths of the seas. O LORD, our Lord, how majestic is your name in all the earth!

In verse 1, we see God the creator in the picture; now take note of verses 4, 5, and 6. In verse 4, the Bible says, "What is a man that you are mindful of him? And the son of man that you care for him. You have made him a little lower than heavenly beings." The term "heavenly beings" there is talking about the angels. Of course, later in verse 6, man is said to have dominion over the works of God's hands. God put all things under man's feet—all sheep, oxen, the beasts of the field and the birds of the air, and the fish of the sea (Genesis 1:25–28). So the angels and man are the two creations of God that have perpetrated and perpetuated evil and will face the consequences of their actions. Two things happened that began the perpetration of evil. It was the rebellion among angels and the fall of man.

Perpetration of Evil

The archangel that began the process, whose desire became the driving force for evil to be perpetrated is Lucifer – the Devil. The story of the fall of Lucifer is in Ezekiel 28:11–19 and Isaiah 14:12–15. Before going into Ezekiel 28 and Isaiah 14, let us quickly look at Revelation 12:7–9:

> Now war arose in heaven, Michael and his angels fighting against the dragon. And the dragon and his angels fought back, but he was defeated, and there was no longer any place for them in heaven. And the great dragon was thrown down, that ancient serpent, who is called the Devil and Satan, the deceiver of the whole world—he was thrown down to the earth, and his angels were thrown down with him. And I heard a loud voice in heaven, saying, "Now the salvation and the power and the kingdom of our God and the authority of his Christ have come, for the accuser of our brothers has been thrown down, who accuses them day and night before our God.

Revelation 12:7–10 summarizes what most theologians believe describes the fall of the Devil. The Bible calls the Devil several names in that chapter: the dragon, the old serpent, the Devil, and Satan, the deceiver of the whole world. He was defeated, and there was no longer a place for him in heaven. So here is the person who first perpetrated evil according to the testimony of scripture. Go back to chapter 12 and start reading from verse 3:

> And another sign appeared in heaven: behold, a great red dragon, with seven heads and ten horns, and on his heads seven diadems. His tail swept down a third of the stars of heaven and cast them to the earth. And the dragon stood

before the woman who was about to give birth, so that when she bore her child, he might devour it.

Theologians believe that the third of the stars of heaven here refers to angels that fell with the Devil. They followed his planned coup d'état. These angels are now the principalities and powers and rulers of the darkness of this age. They are the evil spirits and demons that Jesus gave believers authority to cast out. In a sense, within the context of this book, I see the woman in that passage as all of creation groaning to give birth to the sons of God, which is God's purpose for creation. Creation waits eagerly, in expectation, for the manifestation of the sons of God:

> For the creation waits with eager longing for the revealing of the sons of God. For the creation was subjected to futility, not willingly, but because of him who subjected it, in hope that the creation itself will be set free from its bondage to corruption and obtain the freedom of the glory of the children of God. For we know that the whole creation has been groaning together in the pains of childbirth until now. (Romans 8:19–22, ESV)

See chapters 6 and 7 for details on revealing the sons of God. On the other hand, the Devil waits to ensure that creation never fulfills her purpose and be saved through the birth of the sons of God:

> Romans 8:20—"For the creation was subjected to futility, not willingly, but because of him who subjected it, in hope."

> Ephesians 6:12—"For we do not wrestle against flesh and blood, but against the rulers, against the authorities, against the cosmic powers over this present darkness, against the spiritual forces of evil in the heavenly places."

Ephesians 6 above describes the fallen angelic forces who now operate the satanic kingdom with the Devil to perpetrate, and perpetuate evil in the cosmos. These cosmic powers decided to plan a coup d'état against the Most High God, as we will see in Ezekiel 28 and Isaiah 14. They were trying to overthrow God. They wanted to dethrone God, which was an impossible task. So a third of the angels were deceived. That is why Lucifer is called the deceiver in chapter 12, verse 9. He also deceived man in the garden of Eden. The name deceiver shows us that one of the fundamental attributes and manner with which the Devil perpetrates evil is deceiving created conscious beings by luring them into selfish desire.

So by the simple text of scripture, we have seen here that there was an angel of the Lord who fell and was cast down from heaven. His name is the Devil, also called the deceiver. And he is still deceiving men today. Most theologians believe that, although Ezekiel 28 is talking about the story of a king, it is an allegory describing the fall of the Devil. So let me read beginning from verse 11 (ESV):

> Moreover, the word of the LORD came to me: "Son of man, raise a lamentation over the King of Tyre, and say to him, Thus says the Lord GOD: 'You were the signet of perfection, full of wisdom and perfect in beauty. You were in Eden, the garden of God; every precious stone was your covering, sardius, topaz, and diamond, beryl, onyx, and jasper, sapphire, emerald, and carbuncle; and crafted in gold were your settings and your engravings. On the day that you were created, they were prepared. You were an anointed guardian cherub. I placed you; you were on the holy mountain of God; in the midst of the stones of fire you walked. You were blameless in your ways from the day you were created, till unrighteousness was found in you. In the abundance of your trade you were filled with violence in your midst, and you sinned; so I cast you as a profane thing from the mountain of God, and I destroyed you, O guardian cherub, from the midst of the stones of fire. Your heart was proud because

of your beauty; you corrupted your wisdom for the sake of your splendor. I cast you to the ground; I exposed you before kings, to feast their eyes on you. By the multitude of your iniquities, in the unrighteousness of your trade you profaned your sanctuaries; so I brought fire out from your midst; it consumed you, and I turned you to ashes on the earth in the sight of all who saw you. All who know you among the peoples are appalled at you; you have come to a dreadful end and shall be no more forever.'"

Now when you read that scripture, you will think he's talking about an earthly king. But when you look at it very critically, you will see words like, "You were the signet of perfection, full of wisdom and perfect in beauty." Words like being in "Eden the garden of God...and cast down to the ground or the earth."

These expressions show that whomever the scripture discusses is not an earthly king. What God was illustrating with the story of the King of Tyre happened before man. According to the scripture, Lucifer was the actual ruler (vs. 12, "a king"). He was the guardian cherub (vs. 16).

Revelation 4:6–9 (among other texts in Exodus 25:17–20, Genesis 3:24, Exodus 25:22, Ezekiel 10:1–20, and Hebrews 9:5) speaks about cherubs:

Also, in front of the throne there was what looked like a sea of glass, clear as crystal. In the center, around the throne, were four living creatures, and they were covered with eyes, in front and in back. The first living creature was like a lion, the second was like an ox, the third had a face like a man, the fourth was like a flying eagle. Each of the four living creatures had six wings and was covered with eyes all around, even under its wings. Day and night they never stop saying: "Holy, holy, holy is the Lord God Almighty, who was, and is, and is to come." Whenever the living creatures give glory, honor and thanks to him who sits on the throne and who lives forever and ever.

102

Hebrews 9:5—"Above the ark were the cherubim of the glory, overshadowing the atonement cover."

The cherubs are extraordinary creatures of God created to be very close to the throne of God's grace and mercy and live for the praise of His glory. The Devil was an anointed cherub. He had wings like the angels that covered the throne of God. He was the guardian angel of the mercy seat. I see him as the closest creature to God, designed with precious stone to refract the light of God's presence to all other angels and creations. He was the leader of the angelic cherubs, who sang the praise of God forever. The Bible did say he had all kinds of unique precious stones in his body by creation:

> Very precious stone was your covering, sardius, topaz, and diamond, beryl, onyx, and jasper, sapphire, emerald, and carbuncle; and crafted in gold were your settings and your engravings. On the day that you were created they were prepared. (Ezekiel 28:13)

God designed him to reflect and refract the light of His glory and show the magnificence of His creation in the excellence of beauty. Try to find out about those precious stones—they are beautiful. The Devil was a worshipper in heaven. He was like a "priest" in heaven before he fell.

If you compare Exodus 28:15–22 and Ezekiel 28:23, you will see the similarity in the gemstones of the breastplate of the priest and the creation of Lucifer:

> You shall make a breastpiece of judgment, in skilled work. In the style of the ephod you shall make it—of gold, blue and purple and scarlet yarns, and fine twined linen shall you make it. It shall be square and doubled, a span its length and a span its breadth. **You shall set in it four rows of stones. A row of sardius, topaz, and carbuncle shall be the first row; and the second row an emerald, a sapphire, and a diamond; and the third row a jacinth, an agate, and an amethyst; and the**

fourth row a beryl, an onyx, and a jasper. They shall be set in gold filigree. There shall be twelve stones with their names according to the names of the sons of Israel. They shall be like signets, each engraved with its name, for the twelve tribes. You shall make for the breastpiece twisted chains like cords, of pure gold.

This similarity strongly suggests that Lucifer was a kind of heavenly "priest" that worshipped God in heaven. Lucifer has a musical instrument built into his creation:

Thou hast been in Eden the garden of God; every precious stone was thy covering, the sardius, topaz, and the diamond, the beryl, the onyx, and the jasper, the sapphire, the emerald, and the carbuncle, and gold: **the workmanship of thy tabrets and of thy pipes was prepared in thee in the day that thou wast created.** (Ezekiel 28:13)

The Hebrew word for tabrets is the word *tofe*—which means tambourine or timbrel, suggesting that the movement of the Devil in heaven creates music for the praise of God in heaven.

One thing to note here is that Lucifer's precious stones were probably reflecting and refracting light so much that the rest of the heavenly beings might have been tempted to think of him as the source of glory and radiance (Lucifer: "shining one"). Then he became proud, thinking he was the source of the glory and desired to be God and be worshipped as God (Matthew 4). That *selfish desire* led to his fall. He was just a reflector and channel of God's light, beauty, radiance, and glory—he was not the true light that lightens all men. This error of Lucifer is a call for those who know God, display His glory, excellence, and have tasted of the power of the age to come—an anointing—to beware of sharing in His glory. To ascribe glory to yourself is to plan the way down.

Notice here that this cherub was created perfectly in verse 12: "You were the signet of perfection, full of wisdom and perfect in beauty." He was created good, confirming that God did not directly create evil. What God created was good. Even the Devil, who is the personification of evil, was not created evil—he was Lucifer, the shining one. He became the Devil. He was anointed and blameless in all his ways in the Mountain of God (Ezekiel 28:14–15). He was leading the angels, and he was the anointed guardian cherub. He had all the instruments that he needed to perform his function built into his body. And then if you go a little further, the Bible said he profaned his wisdom. He corrupted his wisdom (vs. 17). He was so perfect, blameless, full of wisdom, anointed, and walked in the presence of God. But he profaned his wisdom when unrighteousness or iniquity was found in him. If you read the KJV, where the ESV says unrighteousness, King James uses the word "iniquity."

Principle of Evil—the Mystery of Iniquity

Let's go to Isaiah 14 to establish something about the fall of the Devil—what was the underlying principle of operation that turned him from Lucifer to Satan, the doer of evil?

> How you are fallen from heaven, O Day Star, Son of Dawn! How you are cut down to the ground, you who laid the nations low! You said in your heart, "**I will** ascend to heaven; above the stars of God, **I will** set my throne on high; **I will** sit on the mount of assembly in the far reaches of the north; **I will** ascend above the heights of the clouds; **I will** make myself like the Most High." But you are brought down to Sheol, to the far reaches of the pit. (Isaiah 14:12–15)

In Ezekiel 28, we read that Lucifer was created with the excellence of beauty until iniquity was found in Him. The big question is "What is iniquity"? I believe that Isaiah 14:13–14 shows what iniquity is.

Iniquity is the desire or will to be God and be worshipped as God. It is the principle of *self*—when you put self on the throne of your life and the throne of other people's lives, when you want it to be all be about you and you alone. Lucifer said, "**I** will make my**SELF** like the **Most High**" (vs. 14, emphasis added).

The Most High is God, and the Devil wanted to make himself like the Most High. Notice how many times "I will" appears between verses 12 and 14. In the ESV translation, there are five. That shows you that the principle of iniquity begins with a desire or the will of self above all else. Therefore, whenever you put your selfish desire above all else, iniquity is found in you. The consequence is that you have set the driving force for evil in place. In other words, evil is a manifestation of self on the throne of your heart. Let's see the progression of how the Devil acted out the first evil:

1. He wanted to ascend.
2. He wanted to be above.
3. He wanted to be enthroned in the highest place.
4. He wanted to stay enthroned over all.
5. He wanted to sit above the clouds.
6. He wanted to make himself like God and be the Most High.

We know from vs. 14 that all these desires began in his heart. It is incredible how powerful are the things that we say to ourself. I see here that the Devil nurtured his desire by speaking to himself. A part of me could see the power of the spoken word in scripture: "Death and life are in the power of the tongue" (Proverbs 18:21).

Just as selfish desire led to evil when nurtured through what is spoken in the heart, you can also nurture good desire through what is spoken—look at Isaiah 14:13–15. One of the ways to reduce the perpetration and perpetuation of evil is for man to reverse how Lucifer began the principle of iniquity. It goes something like this:

> You said in your heart, "God **will** ascend to heaven; above the stars, God **will** set His throne on high; God **will** sit on the mount of assembly in the far reaches of the north; God **will** ascend above the heights of the clouds; God **will** remain the Most High."

Replace "I will" with "God will" and get self out of the picture. We must do this in our hearts, not just with our mouths. We must develop a heart and mouth that is full of God's praise, lifting Him high. Lucifer said in his heart and not just in his mouth. What do we tell our heart? Is it "I will" or "God will"?

What happened to Lucifer was that he was so close to God, who is light with no darkness at all. As the Devil reflected the splendor of God's glorious light to the rest of the angels, he started to think this was all about him. He began to desire to be all in all. Everything began to be about him and him alone.

The desire of the Devil made him lose his place. Of course, he was Lucifer, the Morning Star, the Son of the Dawn, the light-bearer, but he became the **doer** of **evil,** which results from the principle of iniquity, the principle of "I will," the principle of self. But it started from a desire in his heart—the desire to be self-sufficient and worshipped. It is the principle of speaking to your heart based on a desire to achieve something for yourself without God. So the principle of iniquity that led to the perpetuation of evil is the desire to put self first instead of God.

Lucifer did not think about the other angels. He did not think about how his action affected the Godhead. He was so absorbed in himself. The Devil wanted self-honor, self-promotion, self-aggrandizement, self-achievements, and to make Himself God. What is the principle of iniquity that leads to evil? It is when self becomes God. Somebody said when you write the letter *i* and you put a dot on it, you crown "I" as the king. And whenever "I" is crowned as a king instead of God, evil is knocking at your door. Lucifer's great mistake was in not realizing and acknowledging that there is only one true God (Isaiah 40:25 and 44:6).

When selfish desire and selfish ambition have consumed you, although you might be a "Lucifer" and you are currently beaming forth the light of God and singing His praise, Satan is close to your door—you are close to being changed from the son of light into a child of the darkness.

As soon as Lucifer became the first perpetrator of evil, God, the righteous Judge, condemned him to hell—Sheol or Hades:

> Isaiah 14:15(KJV)—"Yet thou shalt be brought down to Hell, to the sides of the pit."

> Isaiah 14:15 (ESV)—"But you are brought down to Sheol, to the far reaches of the pit."

Essentially, Hades or Sheol is the judgment of the Devil. We also know by the testimony of scriptures that the lake of fire was also created for the Devil and his angels. Satan and his demons will spend forever in the lake of fire. God, who is good and wants only good for humanity, must operate righteous judgment to eradicate evil forever in the lake of fire so that the universe He created will experience only good for all eternity. How does this not demonstrate that God is good and He always does good? If you say that God judging Satan and his cohort to hell and the lake of fire is evil, I will want to ask if you think a human judge who sentences a serial killer to life imprisonment is an evil person. Matthew 25:41 says, "Then he will say to those on his left, 'Depart from me, you cursed, into the eternal fire prepared for the Devil and his angels.'"

So from the beginning, God decided that He would judge evil—the Devil will be cast into the lake of fire. According to Revelation 12, Ezekiel 28, Isaiah 14, and

Matthew 25:41, those angels that fell with the Devil are already judged by God. He is just waiting to fulfill His purpose, which we will discuss in chapter 6. God is working everything to the end to reveal sons—sons and daughters of men that will become sons and daughters of God.

From that moment described in this chapter, Satan, Lucifer, became the **evil one**. Jesus was teaching us to pray in Matthew 6. Verse 13 says, "And lead us not into temptation, but deliver us from **evil**." In the ERV, it says, "Don't let us be tempted but save us from the **evil one**."

Before creation, there was no such thing as evil. But after creation, the Devil became the evil one. He became the personification of evil. One way to think about the Devil as the evil one is to think of him as evil incarnate just as Jesus was God incarnate. Therefore, every time you see evil, It is all traced back to the work of the Devil and his demons. After the Devil was judged, he decided he would perpetrate and perpetuate evil in the world so that God's ultimate desire, which leads and works all things for good, would not be accomplished. At that moment, the Devil devised a strategy to prevent the manifestation of the sons of God. The plan was to infect the entire human race with the "virus" called iniquity. We have described the principle of iniquity earlier. Genesis 3 gave us revelational insight into how the Devil infected humans with the "virus" of iniquity.

Perpetuation of Evil

Satan, the deceiver (Revelation 12), deceived Adam and Eve. They both chose to eat the tree of the knowledge of good and evil that was in the midst of the garden. God told them not to eat it, not to know the principle of iniquity that leads to evil. Instead, He wanted them to eat the tree of life to make permanent their sonship. The tree of the knowledge of good and evil embodies the principle of iniquity—the self-life—and the tree of life is the embodiment of the principle of the life of the Son. After eating from the tree of the knowledge of good

109

and evil, man now knew about good and evil. Humans now perpetrate and perpetuate either good or evil. As a conscious being, man has not only the potential for evil but can now have a selfish desire that is the driving force for evil. There is now another source of knowledge outside of God, such that man can now say, "I will be like the Most High." You will notice that in Genesis 3, as soon as Adam and Eve eat from the tree, they start to become self-absorbed and begin to accuse each other.

Just like a computer virus, the way the "virus" of iniquity works is that it reproduces itself in the system and continues to perform the act— with mischievous intent without the knowledge of the owner of the computer. So what did the old serpent, as we read in Revelation 12, do? Here is what he did:

> Now the serpent was craftier than any of that beast of the field that the Lord God made" "He said to the woman, 'Did God say you shall not eat of any tree in the garden?' And the woman said to the serpent, 'We may eat of the fruit of the trees in the garden, but God said, 'You shall not eat of the fruit of the tree that is in the midst of the garden.' (Genesis 3:1–3 ESV).

When the Devil lured the woman to take the tree of knowledge of good and evil, she could have said no to that evil. However, she took it when she saw that the tree was "desired" to make her wise:

> And when the woman saw that the tree was good for food, and that it was pleasant to the eyes, and a tree to be **desired** to make one wise, she took of the fruit thereof, and did eat, and gave also unto her husband with her; and he did eat. (Genesis 3:6)

You can see here also that selfish **desire** is the driving force for evil. After the fall of Adam, God asked them a pertinent question, which I first saw in a significant manner in the early 2000s. I listened to a message by one of the ministers of the gospel who I highly admire and who inspires me a lot, Bro Gbile Akanni (he is a widely travelled Bible teacher who lives in Gboko, Benue State Nigeria leading the Living Seed: Peace House team of ministers). The question is in Genesis 3:11: "And he said, **Who told thee that thou wast naked? Hast thou eaten of the tree, whereof I commanded thee that thou shouldest not eat?"**

Just like the Devil said in his heart, there is a voice speaking inside all of us that triggers the driving force of evil. Is there another source of knowledge outside of God that leads to a different desire? I see here that a voice of iniquity is a precursor to the perpetration of evil. In other words, every time evil is perpetrated, it is always preceded by a voice of iniquity speaking on the inside to that man which, if not countered with the voice of the Spirit, will lead to acting out evil desires. You and I need to ask this question whenever we are about to act "Who told you…" That is how you catch iniquity and hinder the spread of evil. If you find out the voice is not from God's Spirit, you should resist it by speaking to yourself and denying yourself from lusting against the Spirit.

> **But I say, walk by the Spirit, and you will not gratify the desires of the flesh. For the desires of the flesh are against the Spirit, and the desires of the Spirit are against the flesh, for these are opposed to each other, to keep you from doing the things you want to do.** But if the Spirit leads you, you are not under the law. Now the works of the flesh are evident: sexual immorality, impurity, sensuality, idolatry, sorcery, enmity, strife, jealousy, fits of anger, rivalries, dissensions, divisions, envy, drunkenness, orgies, and things like these. As I warned you before, I warn you that those who do such things will not inherit the kingdom of God. But the fruit of the Spirit is love, joy, peace, patience, kindness,

goodness, faithfulness, gentleness, self-control; against such things there is no law. (Galatians 5:16–23 ESV)

The works and voice of iniquity are against the fruit and voice of the Spirit. We will see in chapters 6 and 7 that following the voice of the spirit is how you become a son of God, just as following the voice of iniquity is how you become a child of the Devil.

Other names for iniquity are flesh, human nature, lower nature, Adamic nature, sinful self, old man, the darkness, unregenerated self, old identity, and the likes. I recommend *Becoming Like Jesus* by Bro Gbile Akanni and *The Normal Christian Life* by Watchman Nee as additional resources. You see what happened when the Devil, one of the first conscious beings that God created, practiced evil. He started from a desire that led to pride and self-centeredness. When man also was to fall, it began with a desire that led to pride—a sense of independent knowledge outside of God and self-sufficiency. Every time evil is to be perpetrated, It starts with selfish desire and pride. Every time good is to be done, which is a fruit of the Spirit, there is always godly desire, selflessness, and humility.

Remember, the principle of iniquity is what made Lucifer the Devil. If you go to Psalm 51:5, you read, "Behold, I was brought forth in iniquity, and in sin did my mother conceive me." David made it clear that the entire human race from Adam started to come to this world born in iniquity and evil nature by birth—this is how the Devil continues to spread this "virus" called iniquity to keep evil going in the universe.

Remember we said God alone is good. In Genesis 1, God wanted to pour out and multiply His goodness in creation. For this reason, He monitored His creation to see that all He created was good. On the other hand, the Devil has infected all of humanity with the venom or "virus" of iniquity. So the Devil put in what God loves the thing that God hates. Since God must fulfill His purpose of sonship—see chapter 6—He blessed man to be fruitful and multiply. As humans

112

multiply, according to the promise of God, every single one is born with this "virus" called iniquity, the evil desire, evil intention, and evil nature, or a lower nature, one that is selfish, prideful, self-centered nature. That is the principle of evil. Little will you be surprised that humans perpetrate so much evil in the world when you understand this principle of iniquity. It's everywhere. Isaiah 53:5–6 teaches us that we all have iniquity:

> But he was pierced for our transgressions; he was crushed for our iniquities; upon him was the chastisement that brought us peace, and with his wounds we are healed. All we like sheep have gone astray; we have turned—everyone—to his own way; and the LORD has laid on him the **iniquity of us all.**

Iniquity is the principle of evil or what you might call evilness. For better word choice, there is something in us, by birth, that desires to act against the desire of God:

> **But I say, walk by the Spirit, and you will not gratify the desires of the flesh. For the desires of the flesh are against the Spirit, and the desires of the Spirit are against the flesh, for these are opposed to each other, to keep you from doing the things you want to do.** (Galatians 5:16–17)

There is the desire of the Spirit, which is the kind of desire that becomes the driving force for good. There is a desire of the flesh, which is the desire of iniquity in us, against the desire for good. Consistently we see that selfish desire is the driving force for evil. Another way to think about this is to consider that evil is illustrated or typified as "the darkness." 1 Thessalonians 5:4–5 talks about children of the day and those of the darkness: "But you are not in darkness, brothers, for that day to surprise you like a thief. For you are all children of light, children of the day. We are not of the night or of the darkness."

So from this chapter we see that selfish desire is like the desire of the darkness, the flesh, or iniquity that led Lucifer to become the Devil. He was Lucifer (the light-bearer), the Son of the Dawn, the Morning Star. So every time you see evil being active, it is never the work of God. The Bible says God cannot do evil or be tempted by evil:

> Let no one say when he is tempted, "I am being tempted by God," for God cannot be tempted with **evil**, and he himself tempts no one. But each person is tempted when he is lured and enticed by his own **desire.** Then **desire** when it has conceived gives birth to sin, and sin when it is fully grown brings forth death. (James 1:13–15 ESV)

God is light, and there is no darkness in him. "This is the message we have heard from him and proclaim to you, that **God is light, and in him is no darkness at all.**" (1 John 1:5, ESV)

So in summary, we have seen that every time you see evil being perpetrated, it is the work of the Devil. And the Devil has found a partner in fallen humanity, who are all born with iniquity in them (Romans 5:12–21). No wonder the Bible says we must be born again to become sons of God, which is what God is doing in this world. God is working to birth sons in this world. God's redemptive plan against evil is not for the Devil or the angels because God's plan for sonship is not with the Devil but with humanity:

> Psalm 8:4—"**What is man that you are mindful of him,** and the son of man that you care for him?"

> Hebrews 2:5,9—"**For it was not to angels that God subjected the world to come, of which we are speaking...But we see him who for a little while was made lower than the angels, namely Jesus, crowned with glory and honor because of the suffering of death, so that by the grace of God he might taste death for everyone.**"

God already decided that the Devil and his demons, according to Matthew 25:41, will spend eternity in the lake of fire. But for man, God made a redemptive plan to deal with evil. Jesus Christ became the lamb who was foreordained before the foundation of the world and was slain from the foundation of the world. He took on the office of Christ to fulfill the plan of God to restore man and enable man to partake in His program for creation—the manifestation of sons. The plan included death so that the iniquity of us all will die with Him by one death—the death of Jesus. Through the resurrection of Jesus, we might all be born of God—born from above, so that mankind can become sons of God.

This chapter clearly reveals the origin of the perpetration of evil. Evil was perpetrated by the Devil, his fallen angels, demons, and humanity. There has never been a time that God did evil; neither can He be tempted to do evil! God is good. God is light. In Him, there is no darkness at all. Lucifer became the Devil—the accuser of the brethren, the old dragon, the old serpent. In him, there is darkness. There is no good in Satan—he is only filled with evil. Evilness is his handiwork:

"Whoever makes a practice of sinning is of the Devil, for the Devil has been sinning from the beginning. The reason the **Son of God** appeared was to **destroy the works of the Devil**." (1 John 3:8)

Chapter Six

God's Eternal Desire and Purpose

The Heavenly Father's Quest

Romans 8:28–29:

> And we know that for those who love God all things
> work together for good, for those who are called
> **according to his purpose**. For those whom he
> foreknew, he also predestined to be **conformed to the
> image of His Son**, in order that he might **be the
> firstborn among many brothers.**

In chapter 2, we stated that, although He foreknew evil
was a possibility, God continued to create because He has a
purpose to fulfill that evil could not stop. God's purpose is to
have sons from among mankind. To establish this truth let us
look at the main theme text for discussion in this chapter,
which is Ephesians 1:1–14 (KJV). The following is The
Passion Translation (TPT) of the text:

> Dear friends, my name is Paul, and I was chosen by God
> to be an apostle of Jesus, the Messiah. I'm writing this
> letter to all the devoted believers who have been made
> holy by being one with Jesus, the Anointed One. May
> God himself, the heavenly Father of our Lord Jesus
> Christ, release grace over you and impart total well-being

into your lives. Every spiritual blessing in the heavenly realm has already been lavished upon us as a love gift from our wonderful heavenly Father, the Father of our Lord Jesus—all because **he sees us wrapped into Christ** [in Him KJV] . This is why we celebrate him with all our hearts! And in love he chose us **before he laid the foundation of the universe!** Because of his great love, he ordained us, so that we would be seen as holy in his eyes with an unstained innocence. **For it was always in his perfect plan to adopt us as his delightful children, through our union with Jesus, the Anointed One**, so that his tremendous love that cascades over us would glorify his grace —for the same love he has for the Beloved, Jesus, he has for us. And this unfolding plan brings him great pleasure! Since we are now joined to Christ, we have been given the treasures of redemption by his blood—the total cancellation of our sins—all because of the cascading riches of his grace. This superabundant grace is already powerfully working in us, releasing all forms of wisdom and practical understanding. And through the revelation of the Anointed One, he unveiled his **secret desires** to us—**the hidden mystery of his long-range plan, which he was delighted to implement from the very beginning of time**. And because of **God's unfailing purpose**, this detailed plan will reign supreme through every period of time until the fulfillment of all the ages finally reaches its climax—when God makes all things new in all of heaven and earth through Jesus Christ. **Through our union with Christ we too have been claimed by God as his own inheritance. Before we were even born, he gave us our destiny;** that we would fulfill the plan of God who always accomplishes every purpose and plan in his heart. God's purpose was that we Jews, who were the first to long for the messianic hope, would be the first to believe in the Anointed One and bring great praise and glory to God! And because of him, when you who are not Jews heard the revelation of truth, you believed in the

117

wonderful news of salvation. Now we have been stamped with the seal of the promised Holy Spirit. He is given to us like an engagement ring, as the first installment of what's coming! He is our hope-promise of a future inheritance which seals us until we have all of redemption's promises and experience complete freedom—all for the supreme glory and honor of God!.

To understand the motivation of God or the desire of God for creating anything, it is essential to trace what the Bible said about God and His action before the creation of the universe. There are very few things the Bible said God did before the foundation of the world. Ephesians 1:4–5 shows a couple of things God did before the foundation of the world:

1. The Father loved His Son Jesus Christ and those He chose in Him (Ephesians 1:6, Ephesians 2:4, John 17:23–25)
2. He chose us in Christ (Ephesians 1:3). When God made this choice, He had not created anything. This choice is not about a person in and of themselves but a purpose to be performed in Christ. Hence, He chose us in Him.
3. He blessed us with every spiritual blessing in heavenly places (Ephesians 1:4).
4. God predestined us to be adopted as children by Jesus Christ to Himself based on His **pleasure, which He purposed in Himself** in accordance with His will (Ephesians 1:3, 5, 9).
5. The lamb of God was foreordained and slain for our redemption from evil (Ephesians 1:7, Revelation 13:8, 1 Peter 1:19–20).

The Holy Spirit, in Ephesians 1:4–5, reveals why God created anything. Romans 8 is at the back of my mind as I think of these two verses. Our choice, predestination, and blessedness were in the beloved, Who was with the Father and loved before the Father created anything. God created everything, including consciousness, because God wanted to multiply His Son. God has an eternal desire founded on His love for His only begotten Son. He *must* fulfill this desire, and the likelihood that evil could be possible in the cosmos if He created things could not stop Him from actualizing His desire. God desires to achieve a purpose whose plan is in a mystery—the mystery of His will. That mystery is according to a purpose, and God outlined that purpose in Christ. So the Son whom He loved and for whom all things were created was also given the assignment of the Christ, the Anointed One. Christ is the one who actualizes the purpose of the Father. We were predestined, not in and of ourselves but according to the purpose of God in the Beloved. And God works all things to actualize that will according to that purpose of sonship: "In him we have obtained an inheritance, having been predestined according to the purpose of him **who works all things according to the counsel of his will**" (Ephesians 1:11 ESV).

If you ask me what God is doing right now, He is working all things according to the purpose of bringing many sons to glory. Before God created anything, the text in Ephesians 1 reveals that God made a choice based on His pleasure and desire to achieve His will. With a clear purpose in mind, God hid His plan from everyone (hence a mystery) to actualize that will. Ephesians 1:10 describes what God desired and decided in Himself to do.

We who have believed in Christ have obtained inheritance among those chosen by God in His beloved—sons and daughters of men to be adopted as sons of God. And our adoption as sons follows God's purpose to gather in one (His Son, Jesus Christ) everything he was going to create. If you combine verses 5 and 11, you will see that God predestined us for adoption as children and predestined us according to the purpose of His will. Therefore, God's eternal purpose is to have children like His beloved Son, for which He is working all things. No wonder the Bible says in Romans 8:19:

Everything that God made is waiting with excitement for the time when he will show the world

who his children are. The whole world wants very much for that to happen. (ERV)

For the creation waits with eager longing **for the revealing of the sons of God.** (ESV)

For the earnest expectation of the creature **waiteth for the manifestation of the sons of God**. (KJV)

The entire universe is standing on tiptoe, y**earning to see the unveiling of God's glorious sons and daughters!** (TPT)

All of creation waits with **eager longing for God to reveal his children**. (GNT)

Essentially, God conceived of a plan to have many sons like His beloved Son, and His purpose is so that by the revelation of many sons, He will be able to actualize His will, which He conceived to happen in "the fullness of time." Therefore, God created what we now call "time" to actualize His purpose. In other words, time is also an instrument in the hand of God to fulfill His purposes. Whatever you are going through now and evil seems to be having a field day, wait on God and pray while He utilizes time to actualize His purpose for you. God makes everything beautiful in its time. No wonder patience is an essential virtue of the Christian life. While you wait on God to act in time, redeem the time, for the days are evil! Make the most of the time of waiting to align with what God is working and doing per His eternal desire and purpose, which I will also explain later.

According to Romans 8:20–23, God does not yet eradicate evil in the world because creation is waiting for the manifestation of God's sons—this is crucial and consistent with the argument put forward earlier in chapter 2. God has the power to deliver creation from bondage, but God has a plan involving us who are to be adopted as sons. And God must fulfill this plan and purpose in time, and until the fullness of time (when all of God's sons are completed and have been revealed), God will not eradicate evil yet. If that were to happen prematurely, the purpose of God would be cut short or at least not occur in the fullness with which God wanted it. So evil and evilness will continue as God works all of it in line with His will and purpose of bringing many sons to glory. An excellent way to illustrate this is the parable of the weed and the wheat in Matthew 13:24–30 (ESV):

> He put another parable before them, saying, "The kingdom of heaven may be compared to a man who sowed good seed in his field, but while his men were sleeping, his enemy came and sowed weeds among the wheat and went away. So when the plants came up and bore grain, then the weeds appeared also. And the servants of the master of the house came and said to him, 'Master, did you not sow good seed in your field? How then does it have weeds?' He said to them, 'An enemy has done this.' So the servants said to him, 'Then do you want us to go and gather them?' But he said, 'No, lest in gathering the weeds you root up the wheat along with them. Let both grow together until the harvest, and at harvest time I will tell the reapers, "Gather the weeds first and bind them in bundles to be burned, but gather the wheat into my barn.

God sowed wheat (good) on the earth. The Devil sowed weeds (evil) after God had rested from His works. God decided He would not try to remove the weed except at the harvest time so that He does not destroy His plans to harvest sons from among the children of men—from all tribes, nations, kindred, and tongues.

Before I support this truth with several scriptures, I want to make it clear that, just like the entire eternal plan of God, which will be fulfilled in the fullness of time, anytime God allows what looks like evil in a smaller proportion or magnitude to occur, it is because He is working something to achieve sonship in someone or a group of people.

He is working to reveal His Son to, through, in, and for someone in the right proportion and magnitude that will eventually lead to His will of gathering in one all things in Christ. The parable of the weed and wheat portrays God as an investor and harvester. God is working everything to get the maximum harvest from the world and have as many sons as possible to partake in His glory.

God can allow what appears to be evil to continue if it will achieve the ultimate good of revealing His sons. And every time God decides to respond to faith and show up in His supernatural power to do infinitely more than we can ask or think, it is because doing so follows His purpose of revealing His sons too. Otherwise, God may not act in His supernatural power to change the circumstance. Anything God ever worked, is working, or might work in the future will be according to that purpose and eternal desire. So when God was working to create time, space, matter, energy, and all there is, He was working it as part of what must be to achieve His eternal purpose and desire, as stated in Ephesians 1:5, 10–11.

Motivation for Creation: God's Love for His Son

Love is the reason why God created all things—in essence, the love that existed in the community of the trinity (God the Father, the Son, and the Holy Spirit) and particularly the love the Father has for the Son (although perfect), is what drives and is expressed in the creation of all things. The Father wants to bring many sons to glory—the glory He had with the Son before creation:

> The glory that you have given me I have given to them, that they may be one even as we are one, I in them and you in me, that they may become perfectly one, **so that the world may know that you sent me and loved them even as you loved me.** Father, I desire that they

122

also, whom you have given me, may be with me where I am, to see my glory that you have given me because you loved me before the foundation of the world. (John 17:22–24 ESV)

God wants many sons who might partake of and be to the praise of His glory (Ephesians 1:12). Essentially, God wanted to multiply His Son, whom He loves, as you would like to have that which you love to be everywhere. Creation is the outworking of that love that was already perfected in the community of the Trinity before the foundation of the world.

In a nutshell, God has an eternal purpose based on His good pleasure that derives from His love for the Son. And it would be unfair to question the fact that God has a purpose, a good pleasure, desire, will, and love because we also have all these attributes. In other words, it would not be illogical to conceive of and believe that God has these qualities. We know from the Scriptures that God has these attributes. He has a plan for that purpose that would be actualized in time. God's plan will happen in time as He has chosen that it will happen that way. That explains why it looks as if evil or evilness is still having a field day. It is because God is still actualizing His purposes while keeping evil at bay until the fullness of time (Ephesians 1:10–11).

God's Plan to Deal with Evil—the Manifestation of the Sons of God

God's plan to keep evil at bay while we wait for the fullness of time is the manifestation of sons (includes male and female mankind) in measure, portion, and proportion in different localities all over the earth in various forms. We will discuss these manifestations of sons in chapters 8 and 9.

Evil is the work of the Devil. So it is written: **"The reason the Son of God was made manifest [visible] was to undo [destroy, loosen, and dissolve] the works the Devil [has done]"** (1 John 3:8 AMPC). **"How God anointed Jesus**

123

of Nazareth with the Holy Ghost and with power: who **went about doing good** and **healing all that were oppressed of the Devil;** for God was with him" (Acts 10:38 KJV).

Sonship is the goal of creation. So, whenever, and wherever evil still seems to exist, sonship manifested is how God deals with evil both in time and forever. How great is the manifold wisdom of God that, as He is actualizing His purpose (of producing/raising more sons), He is simultaneously eradicating evil at the same time? The Devil fears the manifestation and revealing of God's sons. Jesus Christ is the Ancient of Days that comes in time as the Anointed One Who will smash all evil in its different forms of existence, both as Jesus of Nazareth and through His universal and local body—the church.

The practical meaning of sonship as it relates to our daily lives and how the church fits into sonship and joins with God to deal with evil in time will be explained and brought home in chapters 7, 8, and 9.

Above all, God demonstrated His goodness on the cross, where evil and good met at the same point, and good came out as the winner on the other side as Jesus rose from death. God did this to give us a foretaste that good conquers evil ultimately.

Manifestation of Sons—the Purpose of Creation

To support the statement that God's eternal purpose is to have many sons, we will look at a couple of other scriptures in Colossians:

> He is the image of the invisible God, the firstborn of all creation. **For by him all things were created, in heaven and on earth, visible and invisible, whether thrones or dominions or rulers or authorities—all things were created through him and for him.** (Colossians 1:15–16 ESV).

124

Colossians 1:16 makes it evident that creation came into existence because of Jesus Christ the Son. We know from Ephesians 1 earlier and John 17:22–25 that the Father loved the Son before the foundation of the world and wanted many sons. God wants to adopt you and me as children. He desires to love us with the same love that He loved Jesus before He created a thing.

> John 17:23–24 (ESV) "… so that the world may know that you sent me and **loved them even as you loved me.** … because **you loved me [Jesus] before the foundation of the world…"**

May you know that everlasting love of God (Jeremiah 31:3) that passes all understanding. Behold such a marvelous love:

> 1 John 3:1a (TPT) — Look with wonder at the depth of the **Father's marvelous love** that he has lavished on us! He has called us and made us his very own beloved children.

Below is my prayer for us, which you can pray for yourself as well:

> For this reason I bow my knees before the Father, from whom every family in heaven and on earth is named, that according to the riches of his glory he may grant you to be strengthened with power through his Spirit in your inner being, so that Christ may dwell in your hearts through faith—that you, being rooted and grounded in love, may have strength to comprehend with all the saints what is the breadth and length and height and depth, and to know the love of Christ that surpasses knowledge, that you may be filled with all the fullness of God. Now to him who is able to do far more abundantly than all that we ask or think, according to the power at work within us (Ephesians 3:14-20 ESV)

In Colossians 1:18, we see that Jesus Christ, the Son of God, took on the assignment of the Christ to partake in our humanity to taste death, burial, resurrection, and ascension to pave the way for us to participate in the same. He did that as the firstborn and the first to partake of everything so that He might clear the way for us to partake in it. He did this to open room for us to experience what the Father has chosen for us, predestined to be partakers of **"in Him"** as our inheritance (Ephesians 1:13–14).

Throughout the text in Ephesians 1, the phrase "in Him" keeps showing up because all that we have and will inherit as part of our predestined purpose is only **in Him**, Jesus Christ, not in us or outside of Him. As we partake of all that He first experienced on our behalf, the life of the Father in Him will fill us. All of God will fill us and all of creation in the fullness of time so that good is all there is since only God is good. The life of God in the Son lives in us (Colossians 1:26), who are the chosen in the Beloved. Another passage of scripture that supports the claim that God's eternal purpose is to have many sons is Romans 8:18–30 (KJV):

> For I reckon that the sufferings of this present time are not worthy to be compared with **the glory which shall be revealed in us. For the earnest expectation of the creature waiteth for the manifestation of the sons of God.** For the creature was made subject to vanity, not willingly, but by reason of him who hath subjected the same in hope, Because the creature itself also shall be delivered from the bondage of corruption into the glorious liberty of the children of God. For we know that the whole **creation groaneth and travaileth in pain together until now.** And not only they, but ourselves also, which have the firstfruits of the Spirit, even we ourselves groan within ourselves, waiting for the adoption, to wit, the redemption of our body. **For we are saved by hope: but hope that is seen is not hope: for what a man seeth, why doth he yet hope for? But if we hope for that we see not, then do we with patience**

wait for it. Likewise the Spirit also helpeth our infirmities: for we know not what we should pray for as we ought: but the Spirit itself maketh intercession for us with groanings which cannot be uttered. And he that searcheth the hearts knoweth what is the mind of the Spirit, because he maketh intercession for the saints according to the will of God. And we know that all things work together for good to them that love God, to them who are the called according to his purpose. For whom he did foreknow, he also did predestinate to be conformed to the image of His Son, that he might be the firstborn among many brethren. Moreover whom he did predestinate, them he also called: and whom he called, them he also justified: and whom he justified, them he also glorified.

Romans 8:19 shows us that creation came into existence for the purpose and goal of manifesting, revealing, and "harvesting" sons of God. The expectation or the reason for creation's existence is the manifestation of the sons of God. Creation fulfills its reason for coming to being when it brings forth sons of God. So the whole creation has been in birth pangs all through time. You could think of the entire existence of creation as a childbirth process. Creation is travailing in pain and groaning in anticipation of the birth of the children of God. And all of those who, within creation, have been redeemed are also groaning and waiting eagerly to see the manifestation of sonship in them.

In a nutshell, everything within creation goes through labor to produce the sons of God, which is the good that God is working all things together for (Ephesians 1:11, Romans 8:28). As all creation goes through these birth pangs under the power of the evil one (1 John 5:19) in the hope of bringing forth the son of God, it seems that in our microcosm of creation with our individual experience of pain and suffering, God might be working something good (sonship) out of us while it seems evil is having a field day—just like a mother in labor experiences some of the most painful moments yet, in anticipation of revealing her child, she rejoices. Jesus, who, for the joy that was set before Him, endured the cross as well.

So from Romans 8, we see that glorifying sons is all that God was doing for His creation. God works *all* things together to conform us all to the image of the Son. Our salvation is toward this hope of sonship as well. So I daresay that every time there is something that looks like evil in and around you and it seems like it is not leaving after you pray again and again to God, God is working something to produce the image of Christ in you. You might ask Him to show you this. I pray that God will open the eyes of your heart to see that even when we do not see with our physical eyes, He is working, and He never stops working all things according to the counsel of His will.

God's Unique Will to Bring Many Sons to Glory

The *will* mentioned in Romans 8:27 is that *singular will* of God—which has a purpose for sons to be manifested. Every other will or desire of God is a subset of that eternal desire of God. In verse 28, I believe the good in that verse is not just talking about good things happening to you. It talks about producing good (the Son of God) in us. That was why Jesus says there is no one good but God alone. So in the strictest sense, I believe the good there is that Christ is formed in us as we conform to His image. And every good thing that happens to us that God considers good is only derived from the fact that His ultimate good is being done in us:

James 1:17—"**Every good gift and every perfect gift is from above, coming down from the Father of lights**, with whom there is no variation or shadow due to change."

It comes from God if it is good and bears semblance to God and His only begotten Son. So for everyone who has received Christ (chosen in the Beloved), everything is working together to make them like the Son of God. Everything God allows and disallows—if it is God actively working—it is for one primary purpose: to conform us to the image of Jesus Christ both in time and for all eternity. The glorification of verse 30 is the full manifestation of the sons of God, the sons of men who bear the semblance and image of the Father.

It suffices to say now that the very Son of God, by whom all things exist, is the very one who took the assignment of the Christ to destroy the works of the Devil. The cross, resurrection, ascension, and second coming make sense in this light—all of those were Jesus's way to fulfill the unique will of the Father.

But We See Jesus

Let's look at Hebrews 2:1–18 to strengthen the fact that God's eternal purpose and desire is to bring many sons to glory so that Jesus will be the firstborn among many brethren:

> Therefore we ought to give the more earnest heed to the things which we have heard, lest at any time we should let them slip…How shall we escape, if we neglect so great salvation; which at the first began to be spoken by the Lord, and was confirmed unto us by them that heard him; God also bearing them witness, both with signs and wonders, and with divers miracles, and gifts of the Holy Ghost, according to his own will? For unto the angels hath he not put in subjection the world to come, whereof we speak. **But one in a certain place testified, saying, What is man, that thou art mindful of him? or the son of man, that thou visits him? Thou madest him a little lower than the angels; thou crownest him with glory and honour, and didst set him over the works of thy hands: Thou hast put all things in subjection under his feet. For in that he put all in subjection under him, he left nothing that is not put under him. But now we see not yet all things put under him. But we see Jesus, who was made a little lower than the angels for the suffering of death, crowned with glory and honour; that he by the grace of God should taste**

death for every man. For it became him, for whom are all things, and by whom are all things, in bringing many sons unto glory, to make the captain of their salvation perfect through sufferings. For both he that sanctifieth and they who are sanctified are all of one: for which cause he is not ashamed to call them brethren, Saying, I will declare thy name unto my brethren, in the midst of the church will I sing praise unto thee. And again, I will put my trust in him. And again, Behold I and the children which God hath given me. Forasmuch then as the children are partakers of flesh and blood, he also himself likewise took part of the same; that through death he might destroy him that had the power of death, that is, the devil; And deliver them who through fear of death were all their lifetime subject to bondage. For verily he took not on him the nature of angels; but he took on him the seed of Abraham. Wherefore in all things it behoved him to be made like unto his brethren, that he might be a merciful and faithful high priest in things pertaining to God, to make reconciliation for the sins of the people. For in that he himself hath suffered being tempted, he is able to succour them that are tempted. (Hebrews 2:1–18 KJV)

To fulfill the assignment of the Father to bring forth sons of God from within His creation, the Anointed One is eagerly waiting for the time when all His enemies (evil, sin, self, the world system of evil, death, sorrow, Satan, and all that connects to him) will be put under His footstool (Psalm 110:1–4). However, Hebrews 2:8 states, "**But now we see not yet all things put under him.**" This is because all of this destruction of evil must happen in time and culminate at the dispensation of the fullness of time (Ephesians 1:9–11)

Hebrews 2:10 shows us that Jesus Christ, the Son of God, partook of our pain, suffering, and evil so that He might bring us to glory. Oh, the manifold wisdom of God that the very one by whom all things exist partook of the suffering of evil so that He might show that He is transcendent and immanent in creation because He is good. He is benevolent, and He feels what we feel; He understands our plight while His purpose is being actualized in time, awaiting the fullness of time.

The very transcendent one experiences one of the highest, if not the highest, evil expressions on the cross. The one (though innocent) who came to save was killed by the very one He was dying for, yet He still demonstrated goodness and forgiveness. At the cross, God showed us that good will ultimately overcome evil. God has now stepped into a world that is under the power of the evil one. There is hope for the world, and there is hope for you:

> For it became him, for whom are all things, and by whom are all things, in bringing many sons unto glory, to make the captain of their salvation perfect through sufferings. For both he that sanctifieth and they who are sanctified are all of one: for which cause he is not ashamed to call them brethren, **Saying, I will declare thy name unto my brethren, in the midst of the church will I sing praise unto thee**. (Hebrews 2:10–12)

These verses show us that God's goal is to bring many sons to glory. It is the reason why creation must be in the first place. And when you combine these three verses with Ephesians 1:12–14, you will see that the true son of God lives daily for His praise and to sing His praise.

God's Redemptive Plan to Undo the Work of the Devil to Still Have Sons Among Men

In God's foreknowledge, although He had to continue with His purpose and eternal plan and will, He solved the problem of evilness in man. God does not want to lose man (the object of His adoption as sons) to evil. God foreordained that His Son, whom He loved (John 17:23–25, Ephesians 1:6), would be given to save men who, without an advocate, would have to endure the same judgment as the angelic being Lucifer who sinned. Since God is just and righteous, man could only be freed after due penalty for sin is paid, and Jesus took it all for humanity:

Ephesians 1:7—"In whom we have redemption through his blood, the forgiveness of sins, according to the riches of his grace."

Revelation 13:8—"And all that dwell upon the earth shall worship him, whose names are not written in the **book of life of the lamb slain from the foundation of the world**."

1 Peter 1:19–20—"But with the precious blood of Christ, **as of a lamb without blemish and without spot:** Who verily was **foreordained before the foundation of the world,** but was manifest in these last times for you."

God has to pay the penalty of man's sin through Jesus Christ so that God can actualize His purpose of sonship with man and yet remain a just God. God cannot deny Himself, so He devised a plan to give His beloved Son as a propitiation for man and for man to be redeemed and reconciled back to Him.

The whole concept of the sacrificial lamb was created and proposed by God to the Israelites because it worked together toward God's purpose for the good of having many sons. We would say that God created the lamb for this primary purpose and other secondary purposes like food and clothing for man, who is the object of His eternal purpose. Christ would become a Man to actualize that purpose and be slain like a Lamb for man's redemption. When the Bible designated Jesus as the Lamb that was ordained before and killed at the foundation of the world, God revealed that the primary reason, with other secondary reasons still connected to the primary, He created what we now call lamb (just as He created time, space, energy, and matter) is to serve the mission of foreshadowing Jesus' death to redeem us all with His precious blood and reconcile us back to God.

Amazingly, I hold it as truth that, in the same vein that God created the lamb and sacrificial animals primarily for foreshadowing the redemption of man, the concepts of the door, shepherd, tree, way, path, and bread help illustrate something in connection to God's eternal purpose of revealing the Son. We must trust God to give us the proper illustration that demonstrates the Son since He created things for that purpose. That is why Christ Jesus is the origin, meaning, morality, and destiny of existence. And my perspective on theodicy fits into this position I hold theologically. We are included in His plan in Jesus, for whom He created all things.

God did not need us, but He included us in His plan for His Son, Jesus Christ, and in His goodness, sent His only Son to die for our evil deeds and sins to redeem us to His eternal purpose. What a good God. What have you done with the death of Jesus? Have you believed and received Him into your heart so that God can adopt you into His family? The following Scriptures confirm that Jesus Christ is the one who was slain to redeem us back to God. So the one by whom, through whom, for whom He created all things became the One by Whom and through Whom redemption came because He loved us in His goodness:

> Revelation 5:9—"And they sang a new song, saying, **'Worthy are you** to take the scroll. and to open its seals, **for you were slain, and by your blood you ransomed people for God from every tribe and language and people and nation."**

> Revelation 5:12—"Saying with a loud voice, **'Worthy is the Lamb who was slain,** to receive power and wealth and wisdom and might and honor and glory and blessing!'"

> Isaiah 53:7—"He was oppressed, and he was afflicted, yet he opened not his mouth; **like a lamb that is led to the slaughter, and like a sheep that before its shearers is silent,** so he opened not his mouth."

John 1:29—"The next day he saw Jesus coming toward him, and said, **"Behold, the Lamb of God, who takes away the sin of the world!"**

John 1:36—"And he looked at Jesus as he walked by and said, '**Behold, the Lamb of God!**'"

God's Son, who has the very nature of God's goodness, dealt with evil by His essential goodness on the cross. So goodness had won from the beginning before anything was created in the first place. Jesus Christ was foreordained before the foundation of the world. God decided before He created anything to have His Son become one of us. As one of us, He would deal with evil. So the very God came out of the same God and was foreordained to enter creation that could become evil so that His ultimate goodness, which is by nature, will have the opportunity to defeat evil in humanity. What a good God He is.

God had planned based on His foreknowledge that ultimate goodness and evilness would meet at some point in time and goodness would defeat evilness, which will begin the winding down of time to eradicate evil permanently. That point in time was the cross of Jesus Christ (foreordained as the Lamb of God). That is why the cross is the center of existence in time. It was there that the Lamb that was foreordained before and slain at the foundation of the world was fully manifested to destroy the work of the Devil, which He began in heaven and continued in the garden of Eden. That supports the text of scripture that says, "To this end was the Son of God manifested, that He might destroy the works of the devil. (1 John 3:8 ASV)

And the work of the Devil is to perpetrate and perpetuate evil, which we call evilness in this book. See how good God is and how loving He is to have gone that far to give the Son, whom He loved and for whom He created everything, to become one of us and die so that evil could be destroyed by His act of ultimate goodness and love. Amazing God—Your goodness pursues us daily!

Synopsis of Why Evil Coexists with a Good God Today

Here is a synopsis of the argument for the coexistence of evil while God is still all good!

1. God must create because of His purpose, desire, and the pleasure of His will.
2. That purpose of God must happen within and at the fullness of time since God wants it to happen as such.
3. The possibility of evil cannot stop God from doing what He proposed to do in Himself the way He wanted it to happen.
4. God must and will still fulfill His purpose and remain all-powerful while evil coexist in time.
5. God planned to deal with evil, which only good can actualize.
6. So God became man. As a man, He used His essentially good nature to destroy evil in humanity—all of this He planned before creating anything because of His foreknowledge.
7. He foreordained this plan before He created anything.
8. Evil only has a field day today because God's plan and purpose must happen in time.
9. However, God is dealing with evil in time as well. The most significant blow that began the winding down of time for evil to be eradicated was actualized at Golgotha (Calvary) when Jesus died for you and me.

The mystery of His will is the mystery of godliness:

> Beyond question, great is the mystery of godliness: He who was revealed in the flesh was vindicated in the Spirit, seen by angels, proclaimed among the nations, believed on in the world, Taken up in glory" (1 Timothy 3:16).

When Jesus said, "It is finished," on the cross, He meant, in a great sense, that the work of God to deal with evilness in humanity was finished absolutely by His death. From the time of Jesus's death, we started to count down to the fullness of time. That is what we call the end times. The end times began as soon as Jesus was resurrected. Everything about the resolution of the problem of evil had been scripted without the actors assigned. God wrote the play, and it will happen as written. Jesus Christ is the director, and all actors are chosen as they are found in the Beloved Jesus Christ.

Predestination is not about individuals but Christ. Jesus Christ was the one who was predestined unto glory as He alone existed pre-creation with the Father and the Spirit. So all of us who believed in Christ are chosen in Him. Outside of Him, we fall out of God's eternal plan and will. It is only in Christ that we are free, from creation's bondage, to become new creatures:

2 Corinthians 5:17—"Therefore if any man **be in Christ**, he is a new creature: old things are passed away; behold, all things are become new."

Ephesians 2:10 (ESV)—"For we are his workmanship, created **in Christ Jesus** for good works, which God prepared beforehand, that we should walk in them."

Ephesians 2:10 (AMP)—"For we are His workmanship [His own master work, a work of art], **created in Christ Jesus** [reborn from above—spiritually transformed, renewed, ready to be used] for good works, which God prepared [for us] beforehand [taking paths which He set], so that we would walk in them [living the good life which He prearranged and made ready for us].

We only become a part of the good works (the goodness of God) that Jesus came to actualize when we are reborn from above in Christ. Since Christ's anointing is for Him to do good, it deals with evil in its different expressions:

Acts 10:38 (NIV)—"How God anointed Jesus of Nazareth with the Holy Spirit and power, and how he **went around doing good and healing all who were under the power of the devil because God was with him.**"

So as we are redeemed and reconciled to be born again in the beloved, we become part of the anointed team to deal with evilness in its different degrees of expression in time. The church (the body of Christ) is one of God's instruments to keep evil at bay as time winds to a close for the fullness of God's plan. We are accepted in the beloved and loved with the love that God loves the Son Jesus Christ (John 17:23–25). We are awaiting the hope of sonship, which is glorification. We are also being transformed from one level of glory to another until we become like the Son.

The more I conform to the image of Christ and help others to conform to the image of Christ, the more I will put evilness at bay. Just like God instructed Adam and Eve to be fruitful and multiply, any time a child of God demonstrates love, heals the sick, raises the dead, and helps the poor and the needy, evil is being pushed back and contained before its ultimate eradication.

Chapters 8 and 9 will speak more to this work of good that Jesus pioneered in the world. In those chapters, we will focus on each of the concepts introduced.

Summary of God's Eternal Desire

God's plan is with humans (Psalm 8:4–7, Hebrews 2:5–12). In other words, God did not plan to make sons out of angels, stars, moon, sun, or other works of His hand, so He chose man, in His manifold wisdom, by His sovereign will.

God purposed for humanity to live for the praise of His name and glory (Ephesians 1:14, Psalm 8:2, 9, Hebrews 2:12). Therefore, God's dominion mandate for man in Genesis 1 was by His sovereign election because man is His choice

(Ephesians 1:3–5). God had purposed in Himself to create a conscious being (whom He called Adam) to put His life in them and make that life permanent as they partook of the tree of life, which is the tree that would make the life of the Son permanent in man. No wonder the Bible called Adam the son of God (Luke 3:38).

God's desire in Genesis is that man—spirit, soul, body—would be consumed by the life of the Son (Jesus Christ), which is glorification (Romans 8:30–31). We know what happened before Adam and Eve could partake of that tree of life. They ate from the other tree of the knowledge of good and evil, and God banished them from the garden of Eden. However, the book of Revelation 21 shows how God ultimately eradicated the evil that became part of man after man ate from the tree of the knowledge of good and evil. God eventually recovered all that was lost in Genesis and made everything new. The book's last chapter deals with this in detail as we look at Revelations 21 and 22.

God had a plan in time that there would be children of men who would become sons of God through faith in His only begotten Son. He chose that this would happen before creating anything by His foreknowledge. God foresaw the fall of Lucifer, the angels, and the fall of man. He did not redeem Lucifer and the angels because His purpose (which He purposed in Himself) is not with Lucifer or angels (see Psalm 8 and Hebrews 2). However, for man, He already made redemption, reconciliation, justification, salvation, and glorification plans before creating anything. Are you reading this but do not yet believe in the Son, Jesus Christ? I invite you to consider putting your faith in Christ. Now is the accepted time; today is the day of salvation. Why would you neglect so great a salvation? Can you see that by this rich plan of God, which He foreknew, He is good to us humans? And it is this goodness of God that leads to salvation. Embrace the Son today and receive Him into your heart to become a child of God. He gave us the promise in John 1:12–13:

But to all who did receive him, who believed in his name, he gave the right to become children of God, who were born, not of blood nor of the will of the flesh nor of the will of man, but of God. .

Summary of Rationalization of the Problem of Evil and Theodicy

- How can you say there is a good, all-powerful God and evil still exists?
- The statement of the problem of evil suggests there must be the possibility that there is a God.
- You cannot define ultimate good if you do not pin it down to God, who is the first cause.
- Realize that when God created things, He made them neutral!
- But they can move toward good or evil if they tend toward God's desire or away from God's desire, respectively.
- Evilness does not have potential if God did not create consciousness.
- The driving force for the perpetuation of evil is selfish desire.
- The first conscious beings God created are angels; one of the angels was Lucifer.
- Lucifer had an "I" desire that made him tend toward evil asymptotically until he became evil personified, so far as any consciousness could conceive of evil within the limitation of the human mind.
- Evilness is moving consciously *away* from God's known parameters and domain (God alone is good) towards Iniquity and the Devil.
- God had purposed in His eternal desire by His good pleasure to create consciousness in whom He would multiply the Son. God loved the Son before the foundation of the universe.

- In His foreknowledge, God knew evil could be perpetrated if He created consciousness with desire.
- He made a provision to deal with evil and continued His plan.
- When Adam sinned, He declared that the seed of Adam and Eve (Jesus Christ the Son of God) would bruise the head of the serpent (evil personified).
- Evil and the potential for or the actual perpetration of evil is not powerful enough to stop an all-powerful God from actualizing His will, desire, plan, and purpose. God is always working, and the possibility of evil will never stop Him from doing His work based on His good pleasure. God has a clear plan to deal with evil every time.
- God turns evilness on its head (since He works all things together for good) and utilizes it to actualize His plan (if the prince of this world had known, he would not have crucified the King of Glory). God also utilized this principle at the cross, where evil was ultimately dealt the killing blow. God used suffering and evil to actualize His plan. It is like the story of Joseph where God used what was meant for evil to accomplish His good purposes.
- So every time someone innocent is going through incessant evilness, it is because God is using evil to actualize His good plan following His eternal purpose. Even when we do not see it, He works all things according to the counsel of His will.

Chapter Seven

Sonship—the What and the How

The Divine Labor Room

Chapter 6 explored God's eternal desire and purpose from the Bible. That purpose is that God wants to make humans sons of God. God's desire and purpose are the reasons why He continues creating, although He foreknew that perpetration of evil was a possibility. This chapter continues that thought to help you understand what it means to be a son of God. Romans 8:14–17:

> For all who are **led by the Spirit of God are sons of God**. For you did not receive the spirit of slavery to fall back into fear, but **you have received the Spirit of adoption as sons, by whom we cry, "Abba! Father!"** The Spirit himself bears witness with our spirit that **we are children of God**, and if children, then heirs—heirs of God and fellow heirs with Christ, provided we suffer with him in order that we may also be glorified with him.

And in Romans 8:28–29, it says,

> And we know that for those who love God all things work together for good, for those who are called according to his purpose. For those whom he foreknew he also predestined to **be conformed to the image of**

His Son, in order that he might be the firstborn among many brothers.

God is making humans His sons—conforming sons, daughters, men, and women to the image of His Son, Jesus Christ. What does that practically mean for you and me as an individual? How do you become one of God's sons today? To thoroughly address this concept, a new book about the size of what you are reading now will be needed. Perhaps, that could be a future project for me. For now, I will provide a summary of what sonship entails and hope that you can do a further in-depth study of the reference scriptural texts and other Christian literature on the concepts that I will highlight.

What Is Sonship?

Sonship is becoming like Jesus in essence and deeds. Do not make the mistake of thinking that becoming like Jesus only deals with the character of Jesus alone. Becoming like Jesus to become a son of God is all-encompassing. It includes receiving and living out Christ's loving nature, personality, volition, thought life, emotions, principles, supernatural giftings operations, servant's heart, and all He does and teaches. Study the scriptures to determine who Jesus was and is—that is the life of a son of God. But what else does sonship mean for you and me?

Now, let us go deeper to other renderings of being a son of God in the scriptures. To be a son of God is to:

1. Have Christ in you (Colossians 1:27, cf. John 1:14–16)
2. Have the resurrection life (Romans 1: 3–4)
3. Live a life of love - even for your enemies (Matthew 5:44–45, 1 John 4:7–8)
4. Know God and receive eternal life (John 17:3–4, John 4:7–14)

5. Become like Jesus by following Him in discipleship relationship (Romans 8:28–29, Ephesians 4:10–16, Luke 9:23)
6. Be of and be led by the Spirit (Romans 8:5,13–17)

Prayerfully study all these concepts above, and you will have a better understanding of what sonship means. A person has attained the maturity of sonship—spirit, soul, and body—when they are wholly transformed to be like Jesus. None of us will be that until we die and resurrect or are translated in rapture—taken up. However, the Bible says we are already sons (1 John 3: 2). If we believe in Jesus, we already have the life of Jesus in us. The full manifestation of sonship is God's goal, and it is the full redemption of our spirit, soul, and body from iniquity and sin—entirely consumed by God's life in our spirit, soul, and body.

Now that we know what sonship means and have listed all the different renderings of sonship in the scripture, your part of the process is to ask yourselves daily which of these various aspects of sonship or elements of the lifestyle of the person of Jesus Christ is God working in you and work it out by faith and surrendering:

Philippians 2:12–13 (ESV)—Therefore, my beloved, as you have always obeyed, so now, not only as in my presence but much more in my absence, work out your own salvation with fear and trembling, for it is God who works in you, both to will and to work for his good pleasure.

Jesus taught us His character in Matthew 5–7. This is the unique character that God may be accomplishing in your souls that makes Him allow the pain and suffering to linger. Your role is to surrender to God and allow Him to work the nature and the Spirit of His Son, Jesus, into you. Let the Spirit of God lead you and conform you to the image of Christ in character, purpose, and mission.

If you are going through pain and suffering or apparent evil and you have not received Jesus, your proper response is to open your heart to receive Jesus now so that you can be born of God to become a son of God.

The following sections deal with steps to becoming children of God and growing to become mature sons of God through conformity to the image of Christ.

How You Are Made a Son of God

The summary in this paragraph is to help you see the big picture that will serve as a basis for further prayerful study.

A person is said to be a son of God when the Spirit of Jesus Christ dwells in them. When there is a divine exchange of life at the new birth experience, a person becomes born again. The life of iniquity, old man, human nature, and evil lower nature is replaced with the life of Jesus, the new creation life—Christ in us, the hope of sharing the glory of the manifestation of God's sons. In the garden of Eden, the human nature and the life of iniquity inhabited man, and the first man became sinful and lost the glory of sonship. Through the death, burial, and resurrection of Jesus, we can now partake of the life of the only begotten Son of God to experience and behold His glory. Christ, by His Spirit, is the foretaste and down payment of our final inheritance in God as His son.

It is written in 1 John 3: 2 that now are we His son, and it does not yet appear what we will be like. But when we see Him, we shall be like him. When we are regenerated through faith in the death of Jesus—also the death of our sinful nature in Him—such that when He died, we died, and He has become our life by the working of His cross and resurrection (Colossians 3:3–4). This is the born-again experience, where the evil nature is neutralized (John 3:1–16) as we reckon the death of Jesus on the cross to be our death and the resurrection of Jesus to be our resurrection into a new life (Romans 6:1–

14). So we begin a new life with Christ Jesus's resurrection life becoming our life by His Spirit. The way God did this is to make Him who knew no sin to become sin by partaking in the drink of the "venom" of our sinful and evil nature so that He became sin (like the brazen serpent in the wilderness). We need to be born again then by looking to the cross of Jesus—that His death is like the death of the iniquity that has been in us by birth:

> Psalm 51:5(ESV)—"Behold, I was brought forth in iniquity, and in sin did my mother conceive me."

> Psalm 51:5 (TPT)—"Lord, I have been a sinner from birth, from the moment my mother conceived me."

Consequently, as the people of Israel in the wilderness, we will live again (John 3:3–16). However, we were dead and dying in sin—the satanic venom of iniquity. In essence, Jesus died, so we died. Jesus resurrected, so we are resurrected with the Spirit of Jesus Christ as our new nature and life. We experience His new nature practically and daily by faith in the Son of God, who lives in us:

> Habakkuk 2:4—"Behold, his soul which is lifted up is not upright in him: but **the just shall live by his faith.**"

> Romans 1:17—"For therein is the righteousness of God revealed from faith to faith: as it is written, **The just shall live by faith.**"

> Galatians 3:11—"But that no man is justified by the law in the sight of God, it is evident: for, **The just shall live by faith.**"

> Hebrews 10:38—"**Now the just shall live by faith:** but if any man draw back, my soul shall have no pleasure in him."

Galatians 2:20—"I am crucified with Christ: nevertheless I live; yet not I, but Christ liveth in me: **and the life which I now live in the flesh I live by the faith of the Son of God**, who loved me, and gave himself for me."

The work at the new birth happened in our spirit. As the Spirit of Jesus is now one with our spirit:

> But he **who is joined to the Lord becomes one spirit with him.** Flee from sexual immorality. Every other sin a person commits is outside the body, but the sexually immoral person sins against his own body. Or do you not know that **your body is a temple of the Holy Spirit within you, whom you have from God**? You are not your own, for you were bought with a price. So glorify God in your body. (1 Corinthians 6:17–20)

We are a tripartite being with spirit, soul, and body. When you receive Jesus through faith that He is the Son of God, Christ now lives in our human spirit by His Spirit with His resurrection life. However, our souls need transformation and renewal to conform to the image of Christ the Son.

The process by which transformation to full maturity of sonship happens daily is as we present our human faculty and body to Jesus. Jesus dwells in our spirit (Romans 12:1–3, 1 Corinthians 6:20, Romans 6:13). We renew our mind, surrendering our will to God's will and subjecting our affections and emotion to His by loving Him above all else and spending time in communion with Jesus. We follow him in discipleship—denying ourselves, taking up our cross (as we die with Christ) daily, and following in His footsteps as recorded in the Bible. We set our mind on the things of the Spirit, which are the things of Christ Jesus:

> If then you have been raised with Christ, seek the **things that are above, where Christ is**, seated at the right hand of God. **Set your minds on things that are above**, not

on things that are on earth. For you have died, and your life is hidden with Christ in God. When **Christ who is your life** appears, then you also will appear with him in glory. (Colossians 3:1–4)

Romans 8:5–6—"For those who live according to the flesh set their minds on the things of the flesh, but **those who live according to the Spirit set their minds on the things of the Spirit.** For to set the mind on the flesh is death, **but to set the mind on the Spirit is life and peace.**"

Philippians 2:5—"**Let this mind be in you,** which was also in Christ Jesus."

1 Corinthians 2:16—"For who hath known the mind of the Lord, that he may instruct him? But **we have the mind of Christ.**"

We take Him as our life and the essence of our being and identity from which we live daily by faith as we believe in him as our life now. The mindset that conforms our soul to the image and likeness of Christ is summarized in Galatians 2:20 and Romans 6:8-11(TPT):

I have been crucified with Christ. It is no longer I who live, but Christ who lives in me. And the life I now live in the flesh I live by faith in the Son of God, who loved me and gave himself for me.

Could it be any clearer that **our former identity is now and forever deprived of its power?** For we were co-crucified with him to dismantle the stronghold of sin within us, so that we would not continue to live one moment longer submitted to sin's power...And if **we were co-crucified with the Anointed One,** we know that **we will also share in the fullness of his life....** So let it be the same way with you! **Since you are now joined with him, you must continually view yourselves as dead and unresponsive to sin's appeal while living daily for God's pleasure in union with Jesus, the Anointed One**.

How Becoming Like Jesus, the Son of God, Practically Works

To grow to become more and more like Jesus, you need to:

1.   Deny or disown self and take up your cross
daily by reckoning that you are dead with Christ (Galatians 5:19–21 TPT; Romans 6:6, 11 ESV and TPT; Luke 9:23 AMPC) and having judged that nothing good dwells in the flesh and the sinful self. Accept God's truth that the old you that was born by your parents has been crucified with Jesus on the cross. Taking up your cross daily then means reckoning, believing, and accepting that you died with Christ:

> Luke 9:23 (AMPC)—"And He said to all, If any person wills to come after Me, let him **deny himself [(a) disown himself, (b) forget, lose sight of himself and his own interests, (c) refuse and give up himself]** and take up his cross daily and follow Me [(d)cleave steadfastly to Me, conform wholly to My example in living and, if need be, in dying also]."

> Galatians 5:19–21—"The cravings of the self-life are obvious: Sexual immorality, lustful thoughts, pornography, chasing after things instead of God, manipulating others, hatred of those who get in your way, senseless arguments, resentment when others are favored, temper tantrums, angry quarrels, only thinking of yourself, being in love with your own opinions, being envious of the blessings of others, murder, uncontrolled addictions, wild parties, and all other similar behavior.

148

Haven't I already warned you that those who use their "freedom" for these things will not inherit the kingdom realm of God!"

Romans 6:6 (ESV)—"We know that our **old self** was crucified with him in order that the body of sin might be brought to nothing, so that we would no longer be enslaved to sin."

Romans 6:6—"Could it be any clearer that **our former identity is now and forever deprived of its power? For we were co-crucified with him to dismantle the stronghold of sin within us**, so that we would not continue to live one moment longer submitted to sin's power."

Romans 6:11 (ESV)—"So **you also must consider yourselves dead to sin and alive to God** in Christ Jesus."

Romans 6:11(TPT)—"So let it be the same way with you! Since you are now joined with him, **you must continually view yourselves as dead and unresponsive to sin's appeal while living daily for God's pleasure in union with Jesus**, the Anointed One."

2.   Follow Jesus: take Jesus as your life. Believe that when He resurrected, His new life is now in you. As you put your faith in the Son of God as your life and identity daily, you will start to become more like Jesus. You will put to death the deeds of the nature of iniquity by the Spirit of the Son that is in you by faith (Romans 8:13 TPT), and you will be transformed from one level of glory to another by Jesus (2 Corinthians 3:14–18). This process of following Jesus is also living, walking, and being led by the Spirit. Galatians 5:16–18, 22–26 (TPT) speaks to this:

As you yield freely and fully to the dynamic life and power

of the Holy Spirit [Walk in the Spirit], you will abandon the cravings of your self—life. For your self—life craves the things that offend the Holy Spirit and hinder him from living free within you! And the Holy Spirit's intense cravings hinder your old self—life from dominating you! So then, the two incompatible and conflicting forces within you are your self—life of the flesh and the new creation life of the Spirit But when you are brought into the full freedom of the Spirit of grace, you will no longer be living under the domination of the law, but soaring above it!…But the fruit produced by the Holy Spirit within you is divine love in all its varied expressions: joy that overflows, peace that subdues, patience that endures, kindness in action, a life full of virtue, faith that prevails, gentleness of heart, and strength of spirit. Never set the law above these qualities, for they are meant to be limitless. Keep in mind that we who belong to Jesus, the Anointed One, have already experienced crucifixion. For everything connected with our self—life was put to death on the cross and crucified with Messiah. We must live in the Holy Spirit and follow after him. So may we never be arrogant, or look down on another, for each of us is an original. We must forsake all jealousy that diminishes the value of others.

Being led by the Spirit starts with being of the Spirit. To be of the Spirit is to focus on the things of the Spirit, which are the things of Jesus Christ always (Romans 8:5, Colossians 3:1–2).

Any time your mind is set on the things of Christ—like the Word of God, prayer, thanksgiving, praise of God, praying in the spirit, and whatever is consistent with the life of Jesus as revealed in the Bible—you are of the Spirit. Trust in God with all your heart and do nothing for your *self* (self-life). Waiting to do what the Spirit tells you to do after hearing His prompting is how you mature to be more like Jesus, the Son of God. Seek guidance and find resources that help on how God speaks by

His Spirit. A starting point is that God speaks by Jesus Christ's life through His written word in the Bible—trust and obey what God says in the Bible. The natural frequency of the Word of God in the Bible is the frequency of the current voice of the Holy Spirit. So let the word of Christ fill you richly in all wisdom—that is how you improve the reception of your spiritual antenna (Hebrews 1:1–2, Colossians 3:15–16, Ephesians 5:18–20).

The more you are full of the Spirit, the more receptive is your spiritual antenna. I hope this radio and telecommunication analogy would help you better understand how to develop your spiritual hearing. Also, the more you obey the written word of scriptures, apply the lifestyle of Christ daily, obey the prompting of and what the Spirit speaks to you, the better you can hear Him: "Take care then how you hear, for to the one who has, more will be given, and from the one who has not, even what he thinks that he has will be taken away" (Luke 8:18 ESV). The Spirit is speaking. The question is do we have ears trained to hear him? "He who has an ear, let him hear what the Spirit says to the churches." Revelation 2:29 (ESV).

3. All these works of God's grace were accomplished by the death, burial, and resurrection of Jesus. But we partake in our experience, of the death, burial, and resurrection life of Jesus as we believe without a doubt that His death was our death, and His burial is ours, and His resurrection is our resurrection. *We partake of all the work that God has accomplished for us freely by His grace through faith in God's truth that we now have Christ in us at rebirth as our life.* The practical way to grow to maturity of sonship is taking Christ practically as all in all to you (Colossians 3:11).

4. As all your mind, will, and emotion have become instruments for Christ Jesus in every respect, you are being led of the Spirit—becoming sons of God. Jesus's life of love, even for your enemies, will start to manifest as the fruit of the Spirit

(Galatians 5:22–23) as you begin to know God more, spending time with Jesus in your inner being and through fellowship with other children of God.

5.   God uses the charismatic gifts described in 1 Corinthians 12:4–11, 12–13, 25–18 TPT, Romans 12:4–8 TPT, and ministry of the gift of Christ in the body (Ephesians 4:7–16 TPT) to equip us. As we fellowship with Jesus personally in our secret place through Bible study and prayer and corporate fellowship with members of the body of Christ, we start to learn of Christ the Son through concerted discipleship.

6.   Your manifestation as a son of God in your locality, domain and spheres look something like what Jesus did in His human life in Israel and what He is doing in the church today. In His body—the church—He is producing the fruits of the Spirit and manifesting His power through the charismatic gift of His Spirit to a dying world under the power of the evil one. More will be discussed in chapters 8 and 9.

God, by His grace, put in us the Spirit of Jesus, legally sealed by His death and resurrection, to produce the fruit of the Spirit as we commune with and know Him more and more. In addition, God promised and poured His Spirit upon us so that we can be filled and baptized with His Spirit and fire to demonstrate the Spirit's power, serving as Jesus's witness on Earth. As we are baptized and filled with His Spirit, the operation of God's Spirit upon us manifests in supernatural gifts. Invade your world with the lifestyle of Jesus Christ (Matthew 5–7), His love (1 Corinthians 13), and service in the Holy Spirit's power (Acts 1:8, 1 Corinthians 12). Your world is waiting for you to manifest God's goodness by His Spirit in and upon you—for the Spirit of the Lord is upon you:

> The Spirit of the Lord is upon me, and he has anointed me to **be hope for the poor, freedom for the brokenhearted**, and **new eyes for the blind**, and **to preach to prisoners, "You are set free!"** I have come

to **share the message of Jubilee, for the time of God's great acceptance has begun**. (Luke 4:18–19 TPT)

In a nutshell, Jesus Christ is in you if you are born again and His Spirit is upon you if you are baptized with the Holy Spirit. Christ in you is your hope of sharing in the glory of the sons of God now and in the time to come—for the time is coming and now is. Give room for Christ to live in, grow in, and manifest the fullness of His life in and through you. Are you ready to become a Son of God?

Become Born Again (Born as a Child of God)—the First Step to Become a Son of God

The new birth experience is how you become a child of God. When you have been reborn, you become a new creation in God, and in this new creation Christ is all and in all:

> He came unto his own, and his own received him not. But as many as received him, to them gave the power to become the sons of God, even to them that believe on his name: Which were born, not of blood, nor of the will of the flesh, nor of the will of man, but of God. (John 1:11–13 KJV)

God is birthing sons every day among men as part of the earnest expectation of creation: "Jesus answered and said unto him, 'Verily, verily, I say unto thee, Except a man be born again, he cannot see the kingdom of God'" (John 3:3 KJV).

God invested His Son into creation as a seed so that creation can release in harvest many sons, and you can be a part of them today. Like a seed, Jesus Christ, the Son of God, died for our sins and was resurrected to give you God's eternal life on the inside of you.

John 3:16 (KJV)—"For God so loved the world, that he gave his only begotten Son, that whosoever believeth in him should not perish, but have everlasting life."

John 12:23–26 (ESV)—"And Jesus answered them, '**The hour has come for the Son of Man to be glorified. Truly, truly, I say to you, unless a grain of wheat falls into the earth and dies, it remains alone; but if it dies, it bears much fruit. Whoever loves his life loses it, and whoever hates his life in this world will keep it for eternal life**. If anyone serves me, he must follow me; and where I am, there will my servant be also. If anyone serves me, the Father will honor him."

How do you experience the new birth to become a child of God? Believe that Jesus Christ died for your sins and was buried and resurrected to give you His life. Believe that Jesus Christ is the Son of God who was provided for your salvation. Confess Him as Savior and Lord with your mouth, and you will be saved:

That if thou shalt confess with thy mouth the Lord Jesus, and shalt believe in thine heart that God hath raised him from the dead, thou shalt be saved. For with the heart man believeth unto righteousness; and with the mouth confession is made unto salvation. (Romans 10:9–10)

You can become a child of God now! 1 Peter 1:23(KJV)—"Being born again, not of corruptible seed, but of incorruptible, by the Word of God, which liveth and abideth forever."

Experience the New Birth

The steps to experience the new birth are as follows:

1. Believe that Jesus is whom He says He is, that He is the only Savior from sin, that His death is for you, and that He died with your evil, sinful human nature of iniquity.
2. Confess that you are a sinner and, in repentance from sin, trust Jesus to forgive you of your sins.
3. Confess Jesus as your Savior from your sins. You will want to ask Him to come live inside you as your Savior and Lord.
4. When you confess that you are a sinner and believe in (trust in) Jesus to be your savior from your sins, you become a child of God and you can know that you are no longer guilty in God's sight. Praise be to God; Christ now lives in you!

As you begin your new life as a child of God, you will want to repent (turn away from) any known sin that comes to mind as you learn more about what it means to live life as a Christian. I doubt you can think of all of them at one time, but it will be a good idea to confess every known sin (as God's Holy Spirit brings them to your attention) by name and ask God to forgive you of that sin. When the new birth has taken place, God's spirit of adoption in Jesus Christ, who now lives in you, will bear witness that you are a child of God. You will confidently say that God is your father by His Spirit in you. It is a miraculous experience where God will give you a new heart and a new spirit after He has taken away your heart of stone: This is the promise of God, who cannot lie:

> Ezekiel 36:25–27 (ESV)— I will sprinkle clean water on you, and you shall be clean from all your uncleanness, and from all your idols I will cleanse you. And I will give you a new heart, and a new spirit I will put within you. And I will remove the heart of stone from your flesh and give you a heart of flesh. And I will put my Spirit within you, and cause you to walk in my statutes and be careful to obey my rules.

Hebrews 8:10-11 (ESV) —For this is the covenant that I will make with the house of Israel after those days, declares the Lord: I will put my laws into their minds, and write them on their hearts, and I will be their God, and they shall be my people. And they shall not teach, each one his neighbor and each one his brother, saying, 'Know the Lord,' for they shall all know me, from the least of them to the greatest.

SECTION 3

GOD'S PLAN AGAINST EVIL ON EARTH

Behold, I Make All Things New!

Chapter Eight

He Went About Doing Good

The Mission of God's Unique Son

Acts 10:38 (ESV) reads,

> How God anointed Jesus of Nazareth with the Holy Spirit and with power. He went about doing good and healing all who were oppressed by the devil, for God was with him.

The Son of God went about being Himself—doing good. The Son of God, who made all things, took on the assignment of the Father as the Anointed One (the Christ), to destroy the work of the Devil:

> "Whoever makes a practice of sinning is of the Devil, for the Devil has been sinning from the beginning. **The reason the Son of God appeared was to destroy the works of the Devil**" (1 John 3:8 (ESV).

As the Anointed One, He showed us what it means to do good—to promote good and reduce, if not eliminate, evil in the world:

> God's anointing upon the life of Jesus, as God's Spirit was poured on Him without measure, was to "go about and do good": "The One whom God has sent to

represent him will speak the words of God, for God has poured out upon him the fullness of the Holy Spirit without limitation" (John 3:34 TPT).

While we wait for evil to be completely eradicated in the dispensation of the fullness of time when the sons of God will be revealed throughout all creation, Jesus—being God and therefore good—went about doing and promoting good everywhere evil is prevalent. Throughout the gospels, Jesus Christ healed the sick, cleansed the lepers, set the captives free, delivered the oppressed and the possessed. He fed the hungry, raised the dead, had compassion on the family of the sick and the dead. Everywhere and every time, all that Jesus did in His earthly ministry was good. He understood that He came to destroy the Devil's works and free the captives. Jesus went about spreading good, removing pain and agony from everyone He encountered by God's Spirit.

Essentially, Jesus demonstrated that God is good by showing God's goodness in human form. He showed that God could do in a measure what He will accomplish in the dispensation of the fullness of time. John 4:23 and 5:25 reveal a principle of scripture that shows us that Jesus did in the here and now what God will bring to culmination in the dispensation of the fullness of time:

> **But the hour is coming, and is now here,** when the true worshipers will worship the Father in spirit and truth, for the Father is seeking such people to worship him…Truly, truly, **I say to you, an hour is coming, and is now here,** when the dead will hear the voice of the Son of God, and those who hear will live. (ESV)

At the end of time, God will wipe away all tears. Death, pain, sorrow, and disaster will be no more. Because the former things shall pass away, and the new will begin (Revelation 21). But Jesus is giving us a foretaste now:

Remember not the former things, nor consider the things of old. Behold, I am doing a new thing; now it springs forth, do you not perceive it? I will make a way in the wilderness and rivers in the desert. The wild beasts will honor me, the jackals and the ostriches, for I give water in the wilderness, rivers in the desert, to give drink to my chosen people, the people whom I formed for myself that they might declare my praise. (Isaiah 43:18–21 ESV)

The time is coming, and now it is. Essentially Jesus's earthly ministry is a foretaste of the kingdom of God on Earth. It was a crusade against anything that caused pain, suffering, illnesses, etc. Jesus's campaign was to destroy the works of the Devil, which is evil. He was giving us the foretaste of heaven on Earth. So He went about doing good. If Jesus was God in human flesh, how is Jesus's earthly ministry not an absolute confirmation to us that God is good? Read the following:

1 Timothy 3:16 (ESV)—"Great indeed, we confess, is the mystery of godliness: **He was manifested in the flesh**, vindicated by the Spirit, seen by angels, proclaimed among the nations, believed on in the world, taken up in glory."

James 1:17 and John 3:13 confirm that good gifts come from above (God's dwelling) and that Jesus is **the only one** who came from above:

James 1:17 (ESV)—"**Every good gift and every perfect gift is from above**, coming down from the Father of lights, with whom there is no variation or shadow due to change."

John 3:13 (ESV)—"**No one has ascended into heaven except he who descended from heaven**, the Son of Man."

The ministry of Jesus Christ was prophesied and summed up in Isaiah 61:1–3 (ESV) and applied by Jesus to Himself as the fulfillment in Luke 4:18–21 (ESV).

> **The Spirit of the Lord GOD is upon me**, because the LORD has anointed me to bring good news to the poor; he has sent me to bind up the brokenhearted, to proclaim liberty to the captives, and the opening of the prison to those who are bound; to proclaim the year of the LORD's favor, and the day of vengeance of our God; to comfort all who mourn; to grant to those who mourn in Zion—to give them a beautiful headdress instead of ashes, the oil of gladness instead of mourning, the garment of praise instead of a faint spirit; that they may be called oaks of righteousness, the planting of the LORD, that he may be glorified. (Isaiah 61:1–3 ESV)

> **"The Spirit of the Lord is upon me**, because he has anointed me to proclaim good news to the poor. He has sent me to proclaim liberty to the captives and recovering of sight to the blind, to set at liberty those who are oppressed, to proclaim the year of the Lord's favor." And he rolled up the scroll and gave it back to the attendant and sat down. And the eyes of all in the synagogue were fixed on him. And he began to say to them, **"Today this scripture has been fulfilled in your hearing**." (Luke 4:18–21 ESV)

If you look at Acts 10:38, Isaiah 61:1, and Luke 4:18, it will be evident that the Holy Spirit is the agent of good. If the Holy Spirit is the Spirit of God, what it means then is that God's essence and ruling character is good.

While we are waiting for the complete eradication of evil in all of creation, Jesus began God's end of time plan to promote and keep good on the go. Unlike the anointed cherub that perpetrated evil, Jesus Christ is the Anointed Son of Man that performs and spreads the virtue of good to demonstrate that God is good and, in Him, there is no evil at all. He was anointed with God's Spirit without measure. If you read Acts 10:38, it is written that all that Jesus did was possible because God was with Him. So if Jesus went about doing good, it means that God was with Him to promote and do good because God is good. Jesus's earthly ministry, characterized by doing good, demonstrates that while God unfolds His eternal purposes and plans, He is currently dealing with evil—pain and suffering, death, and disaster that evil brings to people. Everywhere Jesus went, He was doing good. He was using the Holy Spirit's power to deliver and heal all those oppressed by the Devil, whose work is evil. In chapter 5, we discussed the fall of the Devil as a precursor to the perpetration of evil. We attributed all evil to the Devil, who is the doer of evil. So it is the work of the Devil when people are oppressed, possessed by demons, or experience pain and all forms of oppression.

Jesus's earthly ministry started after surviving the temptations in the wilderness, where He showed that the Devil has nothing of Himself in him or power over Him: "I will not talk with you much longer. **The ruler of this world is coming. He has no power over me**" (John 14:30 ERV). Although the whole world is under the power of the evil one, Jesus transcends it—showing that Jesus, God in the human form, is essentially good and cannot be overcome by evil.

Jesus went out, according to Luke's account of His temptations in Luke 4, in the power of the Holy Spirit. At that point, people started to notice Him everywhere as He taught and preached the good news. In Luke 4:16, He went to Nazareth, and as was the custom of the people on Sabbath day, Jesus found the scroll, which would be like the Bible in our day, and He started to read from that scroll (Luke 4:18–21). Jesus's ministry was to do good and to proclaim goodness. Luke 4:21 strongly affirms that Jesus's earthly ministry can be summarized as such—going about doing good and spreading good. Let's have a little peep into the good things Jesus did in His lifetime, which is also available for you today if you believe in Jesus the Son of God.

While in the human body, Jesus did many good works. Jesus helped to remove shame at a wedding feast by turning water into wine (John 2:1-11). He healed the nobleman's son (John 4:46-47), helped Peter's fishing business (Luke 5:1-11), cast out an unclean spirit (Mark 1:23-28), and healed Peter's mother-in-law of a fever (Mark 1:30-31). Jesus cleansed and healed a leper (Mark 1:40-45). Jesus healed the centurion's servant (Matthew 8:5-13) and raised a widow's son from the dead (Luke 7:11-18). Jesus calmed the storm (Matthew 8:23-27), cured two demoniacs (Matthew 8:28-34), and healed a person with paralysis (Matthew 9:1-8). Jesus raised the ruler's daughter from the dead (Matthew 9:18-26), cured the woman with an issue of blood (Luke 8:43-48) opened the eyes of two blind men (Matthew 9:27-31). He loosened the tongue of a man who could not speak (Matthew 9:32-33). Jesus healed an invalid man at the pool called Bethesda (John 5:1-9), restored a withered hand (Matthew 12:10-13), and cured a demon-possessed man (Matthew 12:22). In addition, He fed at least five thousand people (Matthew 14:15-21), healed a woman of Canaan (Matthew 15:22-28), and cured a deaf and mute man (Mark 7:31-37). My lord Jesus fed at least four thousand people (Matthew 15:32-39), caused the eyes of a blind man to be opened (Mark 8:22-26), and delivered a demon-possessed boy (Matthew 17:14-21). Furthermore, Jesus opened the eyes of a man born blind (John 9:1-38) and cured a woman of eighteen years of affliction (Luke 13:10-17). He healed a man of dropsy (Luke 14:1-4), cleansed ten lepers (Luke 17:11-19), and raised Lazarus from the dead (John 11:1-46). In another place, Jesus opened the eyes of two blind men (Matthew 20:30-34). He restored the ear of the high priest's servant who came to arrest him after Peter had cut it off (Luke 22:50-51). Above all, Jesus rose from the dead (Luke 24:5-6). He provided for Peter's fishing business again after His resurrection and Peter had denied Him (John 21:1-14).

So throughout the ministry of Jesus, He removed the pain, hunger, and suffering from people—all of these were pointing to the fact that, even when God was in human form,

164

God kept doing good. God, through Jesus's earthly ministry, kept yelling at us, "I am good, I only do good, I go about doing good, and there is no evil in me."

If you or someone you know is in pain, suffering, in poverty, someone who is oppressed or possessed by a demon, or having a sickness, take their issue to Jesus in prayer or to His followers and messengers. The Bible said, "Whosoever shall call upon the name of the Lord shall be saved." (Romans 10:13 KJV). Like all the people in the stories we have mentioned, you can also go to Jesus, who is still alive today as the life-giving Spirit. Pray to Him and ask Him to heal, deliver, and rescue you from your oppression, pain, and captivity. The Bible did say that the captives shall be set free. It doesn't matter what you're going through. It doesn't matter what your profession is; God is so good. He will hear your cry. So do not think God is evil amid your woes. God is good, and He demonstrates it through the ministry of Jesus.

You will also see in the next chapter that Jesus continues His good works in His body, the church. God is so good. Jesus was anointed to do good, and He further anointed the church to do greater good than He did during His earthly ministry. All of the good works that believers and disciples of Jesus have done in the world—like building schools, hospitals, feeding the poor, healing the sick, casting out the Devil, and much more—are a testament to the fact that God is good.

> **Truly, truly, I say to you, whoever believes in me will also do the works that I do; and greater works than these will he do, because I am going to the Father.** Whatever you ask in my name, this I will do, that the Father may be glorified in the Son. If you ask me anything in my name, I will do it. (John 14:12–14 ESV)

Every day Jesus woke up during His earthly ministry, He was preoccupied with doing good, which shows that the will of the Father for all of us is good.

The purpose of this chapter is to show you that God is good through the life of Jesus Christ of Nazareth—God incarnate. And I daresay that God has been good to you, even if you do not see it. Even now, He is rising on your behalf. I mean, at this moment, God wants to destroy the work of the Devil in your life. Do you want to partner with God through faith today? Believe Him for the impossible right now and see what the good Lord can and will do. Embrace Him today. If you have not given your heart to Jesus, meaning you have never known Him to become a child of God, you have an opportunity right here and now to come to God and receive Jesus into your heart. You can freely say to God,

> You do love me that you send your only son as a gift so that I can experience all your goodness. I don't just want to experience your goodness as a gift, giving me to ease my pain and suffering and heal my disease and sickness. I want to experience the *shalom* and the fullness of your life. So I believe that Jesus died for my sins. And that He rose from the dead to give me a new life. I confess him as Lord and Savior, and I proclaim Jesus as your only begotten Son, and I open my heart for Jesus to come and dwell from today.

John, in his gospel, said that books that fill the entire world cannot contain all the good things that Jesus did in His lifetime:

> That follower is the one who is telling these things. He is the one who has now written them all down. We know that what he says is true. **There are many other things that Jesus did. If every one of them were written down, I think the whole world would not be big enough for all the books that would be written.** (John 21:24–25 ERV)

Doing good was for Him like eating food is for us: "Jesus said, 'My food is to do what the one who sent me wants me to do.

My food is to finish the work that he gave me to do'" (John 4:34 (ESV).

Just as Jesus did good for all these people in Galilee, Judea, Nazareth, and Jerusalem, He is still doing good today. If you can also come to Jesus during your time of trial, test, temptation, suffering, pain, sicknesses and diseases, and any form of oppression, He will heal you and deliver you from all captivity and oppression by His supernatural power. Certain people claim faith in Jesus today but believe that the supernatural work of God like healing and miracles are no longer for today. I'm afraid I vehemently disagree with that view. As we will learn in chapter 9, Jesus continues His earthly ministry through the Holy Spirit today within the body of Christ. Do you need healing? Do you need a miracle, deliverance, etc.? Find a place to call on Jesus today and ask Him to step into your situation, and, keeping with His nature and eternal purpose, He will do you good, and you will be free, healed, and delivered in Jesus's name. Our God is a God of miracles and supernatural wonders and intervention, even today. He must be because He is good, and He has enormous power at His disposal. Come to Him today. The promise of God to you through Jesus is "Whatever you ask in my name, this I will do, that the Father may be glorified in the Son. If you ask me anything in my name, I will do it." (John 14:13–14 ESV)

Chapter Nine

As the Father Sent Me, So Send I You

Expansion of the Unique Son's Mission by the Sons of God

An expression of the commission of the sons of God, the body of Christ, is found in John 20:19–23 and Luke 10:17–20:

> On the evening of that day, the first day of the week, the doors being locked where the disciples were for fear of the Jews, Jesus came and stood among them and said to them, "Peace be with you." When he had said this, he showed them his hands and his side. Then the disciples were glad when they saw the Lord. Jesus said to them again, **"Peace be with you. As the Father has sent me, even so I am sending you."** And when he had said this, he breathed on them and said to them, **"Receive the Holy Spirit.** If you forgive the sins of any, they are forgiven them; if you withhold forgiveness from any, it is withheld." (John 20:19–23 ESV)

> The seventy-two returned with joy, saying, "Lord, even the demons are subject to us in your name!" And he said to them, "I saw Satan fall like lightning from heaven. Behold, I have given you authority to tread on serpents and scorpions, and over all the power of the enemy, and nothing shall hurt you. Nevertheless, do not rejoice in

this, that the spirits are subject to you, but rejoice that your names are written in heaven." (Luke 10:17–20 ESV)

From the beginning of this book to chapter 8, we discussed the problem of evil. We rationalized why there is no mutual exclusivity between a good, benevolent God and the existence of evil. And we argued that both are possible simultaneously, with the caveat that God has a plan to eradicate evil ultimately.

In the last chapter, we focus on the life and ministry of Jesus as the full embodiment of the Father here on Earth. And one thing we notice about Him is that He went about doing good (Acts 10:38). Jesus did all of the things recorded in the gospel—the miracles, healings, casting out of devils, and all the things He did to bring hope to people because God anointed Him by the Holy Spirit without measure, and God was with Him. By the power of God, who is essentially good, Jesus did good and delivered people from the oppressions of the Devil. In the same vein, anywhere the anointing of the person of the Holy Spirit and God's presence is, good can be effectuated in unity with His desire. Let us read the earlier part of the scripture in John 20 to continue our discourse:

But Mary stood weeping outside the tomb, and as she wept she stooped to look into the tomb. And she saw two angels in white, sitting where the body of Jesus had lain, one at the head and one at the feet. said to her, "Woman, why are you weeping?" She said to them, "They have taken away my Lord, and I do not know where they have laid him." Having said this, she turned around and saw Jesus standing, but she did not know that it was Jesus. Jesus said to her, "Woman, why are you weeping? Whom are you seeking?" Supposing him to be the gardener, she said to him, "Sir, if you have carried him away, tell me where you have laid him, and I will take him away." He said to her, "Mary." She turned and said to him in Aramaic, "Rabboni!" (which means Teacher). **Jesus said to her, "Do not cling to me, for I have not yet**

ascended to the Father; but go to my brothers and say to them, 'I am ascending to My Father and your Father, to My God and your God.'" Mary Magdalene went and announced to the disciples, "I have seen the Lord"—and that he had said these things to her. (John 20:11–18 ESV)

You will see that Mary came to the tomb of Jesus, the Anointed One. The one who was anointed to do good was now dead. In a sense, the world's hope for good was now over. If we see Mary as a type of creation, her state represented the state of hopelessness for existence; all hope of liberty seemed lost. It appeared that the light of the world was now shrouded in permanent darkness—the essence of good in the world was gone.

The earnest expectation of creation, the Son of God, was now dead—it seemed creation would now be thoroughly permeated to the maximum by evil. When Mary finally found out that Jesus was resurrected, that hope was now alive, Jesus gave this critical statement: "Jesus said to her, "Do not cling to me, for I have not yet **ascended to the Father;** but go to **my brothers** and say to them, 'I am ascending to **My Father** and **your Father,** to **My God and your God**'" (John 20:17 ESV).

At that point, Jesus made it clear that creation is at the threshold of the fulfillment of the eternal purpose of God—that Jesus would be the firstborn among many brethren. Jesus revealed that the sons of men would be sons of God—though they are the creation of God, they would become sons of God. God would be a Father to them as He is to Jesus. Jesus told Mary, as if to say He was announcing to all of creation, that her expectation was now beginning to manifest. The manifestation of the sons of God is here. He revealed that just as God was His Father, God is now their Father, and the Holy Spirit is now available for them as He was to manifest their sonship.

Biblical Sons Are Sent—Male and Female Alike

I want to clarify that when we talk about sonship throughout this book, we are not dealing with it from the concept of the male gender. As you can see here, Jesus spoke to Mary, a female, and said "my Father" and "your Father." So sonship is simply having the eternal life of God in you to be a child of God. Jesus is now showing us that the beginning of the fulfillment of God's purpose, for which He allowed evil, is now upon us. Mary went and announced to the other disciples. She said, "I have seen the Lord," which began a new chapter in God's plan to eradicate evil.

The thesis of this book centers around the fact that God's quest for children or sons led Him to create the universe, and He allowed evil to still be in existence because He has not harvested the fullness of sons from the earth. In John 20:19–23, Jesus took the attention away from Himself to those who are His brothers and sisters as mentioned in John 20:17. These brethren of Jesus are the first harvest of sons who are now part of the family of God as the new carrier of the commission to go about doing good.

Just as God anointed Jesus of Nazareth with the Holy Spirit and power and He went about doing good, so He said to these sons, "Just as the Father had sent me to go about doing good, I am sending you also."

In the ESV, this verse reads: "Jesus said to them again, "Peace be with you. As the Father has sent me, **even so** I am sending you." The scriptures also say:

> Hebrews 10:7 (ESV)—"Then I said, 'Behold, **I have come to do your will**, O God, as it is written of me in the scroll of the book.'"

> Romans 8:27–28 (ESV)—"And he who searches hearts knows what is the mind of the Spirit, because the Spirit intercedes for the saints according to **the will of God.** And we know that for those who love God **all things**

171

work together for good, for those **who are called according to his purpose.**"

Ephesians 1:11–12 (ESV)—"In him we have obtained an inheritance, having been predestined **according to the purpose of him who works all things according to the counsel of his will,** so that we who were the first to hope in Christ might be to the praise of his glory."

Jesus's commitment to the Father's will, which He works toward good, demonstrates that God is good and only does good. Therefore, it's not just a Christian cliché when we say God is good and He only does good. It is founded on the principle of scripture in Romans 8:27–28 and Ephesians 1:11. God works all things according to the counsel of His will by working everything together for good.

Just as the Father sent Jesus to do His goodwill, there is a commission on the church. There is a commission on every disciple of Jesus to go into the world and do good. One of God's ways of eradicating evil in a locality and keeping evil at bay in the universe is the church. In Matthew 10:5–8 (ESV), we read:

> These twelve Jesus sent out, instructing them, "Go nowhere among the Gentiles and enter no town of the Samaritans, but go rather to the lost sheep of the house of Israel. And proclaim as you go, saying, 'The kingdom of heaven is at hand.' **Heal the sick, raise the dead, cleanse lepers, cast out demons. You received without paying; give without pay.**

Jesus put the same commission He had upon His disciples to be the carrier and the conveyor of God's goodness to the world. Sickness is evil. Death is evil. Leprosy is evil, and demons are evil. So when we cast out demons and cleanse the lepers and raise the dead and heal the sick by the authority of Jesus, we are doing what the Father sent Jesus to do in the world. So whenever you see evil, the church must be present there to be the conveyor of good. See Luke 10:17–20 (ESV):

> The seventy-two returned with joy, saying, "Lord, even the demons are subject to us in your name!" And he said to them, "I saw Satan fall like lightning from heaven. **Behold, I have given you authority to tread on serpents and scorpions, and over all the power of the enemy, and nothing shall hurt you.** Nevertheless, do not rejoice in this, that the spirits are subject to you, but rejoice that your names are written in heaven."

We see that just as Jesus cast out the Devil and God cast out Satan to the earth from heaven, we can also cast out devils. God has given the church authority to make disciples and do good without fearing any physical or demonic snake and scorpion.

It hurts when serpents and scorpions bite; they release venom, poison, and harmful substances into the human body, causing pain, sickness, and death, which are manifestations of evil in the world. And Jesus says when you see serpent-like and scorpion-like experiences in people's lives, He has given us authority to trample over all the power of the enemy. Who is the enemy? The archenemy of God's goodness in this world is Satan—he is the mastermind of all evil in this world. God has delegated authority to the church by Jesus's commission to overcome evil's power as we promote goodness. We exercise our authority by the spoken word and prayer. I am particularly encouraged when I read these verses like this because He didn't say, "I have given you authority over *some* of the power of the enemy. It says "over *all*" the power of the enemy. And I believe it, and I hope you believe it as well. The church is God's instrument, agent, and conveyor of good in this world and the destroyer of evil in this world. Isn't that beautiful?

If we go back to John 20:21–22 (ESV), Jesus gave our commission:

Jesus said to them again, "Peace be with you. As the Father has sent me, even so I am sending you." And when he had said this, he breathed on them and said to them, **"Receive the Holy Spirit."**

When Jesus was going about doing good, as recorded in Acts 10:38, it was because the Holy Spirit anointed Him. In the same way, Jesus also gave the Holy Spirit to the disciples, who were now members of the body of Christ. Since the Holy Spirit was now in His disciples, they could also go about doing good and performing more wondrous works than Jesus did.

Empowered by the Holy Spirit

How important then is the ministry of the Holy Spirit in the life of a believer. The Holy Spirit is the one who does the work of God through the believers. The disciples did a lot of good as recorded through the book of Acts of the Apostles, which some think should be called the Acts of the Holy Spirit in the Apostles. Read the book of Acts if you want to understand what the church should be doing in the world. You will see that we should be doing similar supernatural and humanitarian works like Jesus did.

The early disciples—sons of God—went about doing good with God's Holy Spirit anointing—they healed the sick and the disabled, and they made room to pray to receive the Holy Spirit's new experience. And when there was a complaint in the church that some people were not being treated well—like discrimination in the welfare distribution—the church stepped in and created ways to relieve them of that pain. The sons of God raised the dead back to life. All of the good things that the church recorded in Acts and the epistles are God's display of His goodness.

In Acts 1:8 (ESV), we read: "But you will receive power when the Holy Spirit has come upon you, and you will be my witnesses in Jerusalem and in all Judea and Samaria, and to the end of the earth."

Jesus showed that the Holy Spirit is given to the church for the church to be the conveyor of good. The call of this chapter is that you become the instrument of good in your neighborhood, in your school, in your church, and in your place of work. You can be the instrument and the conveyor of good where you are. We have the authority of Jesus by the Holy Spirit to be the agent of good in the world. Anywhere Jesus went, He was doing good. We have the same commitment to do good and show that our heavenly Father is good.

Some evil is waiting for you to manifest as sons of God to destroy it. May you be filled with the Holy Spirit so that you can join God to destroy the works of the Devil. All problems, evil, pain, suffering, calamities, and disasters can be resolved, turned to good, relieved, and stopped by the power of the Holy Spirit in believers and the authority we have in Jesus:

Luke 10:19 (NIV)—"I have given you authority to trample on snakes and scorpions and to **overcome all the power of the enemy**; nothing will harm you."

Mark 16:15–18 (ESV)—"And he said to them, 'Go into all the world and proclaim the gospel to the whole Creation. Whoever believes and is baptized will be saved, but whoever does not believe will be condemned. **And these signs will accompany those who believe: in my name they will cast out demons; they will speak in new tongues; they will pick up serpents with their hands; and if they drink any deadly poison, it will not hurt them; they will lay their hands on the sick, and they will recover.' And Jesus came and said to them,** 'All authority in heaven and on earth has been given to me.'"

Matthew 28:19, 20 (ESV)—"Go therefore and make disciples of all nations, baptizing them in the name of the Father and of the Son and **of the Holy Spirit,** teaching them to observe all that I have commanded you. And behold, **I am with you always,** to the end of the age."

These scriptures show us that, through the Holy Spirit within and upon the sons of God (members of the body of Christ), God is with us to do good as He was with Jesus (Act 10:38). The sons of God possess the same authority that Jesus had by grace. We have obtained, by His grace, the same legal position that Jesus has over all dominion and power and principalities:

> For this reason, because I have heard of your **faith in the Lord** Jesus and your **love toward all the saints**, I do not cease to **give thanks** for you, remembering you in my **prayers,** that the God of our Lord Jesus Christ, the Father of glory, may give you the **Spirit of wisdom and of revelation in the knowledge of him,** having the eyes of your hearts enlightened, that you may know what is the hope to which he has called you, what are the riches of his glorious inheritance in the saints, and what is the **immeasurable greatness of his power toward us who believe, according to the working of his great might that he worked in Christ when he raised him from the dead and seated him at his right hand in the heavenly places, far above all rule and authority and power and dominion, and above every name that is named, not only in this age but also in the one to come. And he put all things under his feet and gave him as head over all things to the church,** which is his body, the fullness of him who fills all in all. (Ephesians 1:15–23 ESV)

Jesus has been given all authority, and that authority makes all things come under His feet. But He will operate that power and authority through the church. As members of the body of Christ, we have the life of Jesus in us (Colossians 3:1–4). We have the life of the Son of God. Therefore we have the power and the authority of the Son of God as we are sitting with him "**far above all rule and authority and power and dominion, and above every name that is named, not only in this age but also in the one to come.**" (Ephesians 1:21 KJV)

Therefore, like a judge sitting on the throne of judgment over criminals, the sons of God have the power and authority today to pass judgment on evil, pain, suffering, sickness, disaster, oppressions, possessions by demons, and all the things that are on Earth that stand against God's plan for creation. We can command and demand that tumors go, cancer be healed, and arthritis leave. We can give thanks to God and pray for lupus to disappear, and we can ask for the blind to see, the lame to walk, the lepers to be cleansed, for HIV to disappear, for COVID to die. We can ask for a breakthrough for the sons of God to have access to expand God's kingdom, plan, and purposes. By the authority of Jesus, which He now made available for all of us who are sons of God and any others who would be born again, we can stop evil and bring about change to impossible situations. All we need is faith in the power of Jesus by the Holy Spirit: "'If you can'?" said Jesus. "Everything is possible for one who believes" Mark 9:23 (NIV).

God has given Jesus all authority in heaven and on Earth and under the earth to the church:

> Have this mind among yourselves, which is yours in Christ Jesus, who, though he was in the form of God, did not count equality with God a thing to be grasped, but emptied himself, by taking the form of a servant, being born in the likeness of men. And being found in human form, he humbled himself by becoming obedient to the point of death, even death on a cross. **Therefore God has highly exalted him and bestowed on him the name that is above every name, so that at the name of Jesus every knee should bow, in heaven and on earth and under the earth, and every tongue confess**

that Jesus Christ is Lord, to the glory of God the Father. (Philippians 2:5–11 ESV)

Are you going through a bad situation? Are you suffering and it is not going away? Are you in a complicated ordeal that has almost killed you? Perhaps your case appears hopeless and impossible; you need the Holy Spirit and the ministration of the Holy Spirit through faith and prayer. Bring your case before Jesus and His church. Let God's people agree in prayer with you. I believe without a doubt that your situation will change, and God will also change you in the process to conform you to the image of Christ, His Son. Persevere in the place of prayer with the saints, and miracles and breakthroughs will come your way on this earth. As you wait for the anointing on the sons to break the yoke, while you wait to be satisfied by the promise of His word, give Him thanks and know that He is good and that He is working all things together for good.

Find a place where you can start to pray and ask the Father to give you the Holy Spirit. When the church is filled with the Holy Spirit, we will be the witness of Jesus, who went about doing good. Do you want to be filled with the Spirit? Do you want to be baptized with the Holy Spirit, with power from on high that you can do what the apostles did in the book of Acts, empowered to destroy the work of the Devil? That problem and evil in your neighborhood, in your family, in your city, in your streets, in your school, in your place of work, etc., is waiting for you to manifest as a son of God. You may want to bow your heart and say, "Holy Spirit, I need you. Holy Spirit, I want you." He has promised, and He will never fail: "If you then, though you are evil, know how to give good gifts to your children, **how much more will your Father in heaven give the Holy Spirit to those who ask him!**" (Luke 11:13 NIV)

Comparing Matthew 7:11 (NIV): "If you, then, though you are evil, know how to give good gifts to your children, how much more will your Father in heaven give **good gifts** to those who ask him!", You will see that what the Bible called good here is the Holy Spirit. And read Luke 11:9 (NLT): "And so I tell you, keep on asking, and you will receive what you ask for. Keep on seeking, and you will find. Keep on knocking, and the door will be opened to you." So the good that God gives, that He wants us to ask and keep asking for, seek and keep seeking for, knock on doors, and keep knocking doors for more of is the Holy Spirit. Hallelujah.

As I write this book, it is becoming clear that if men who are regenerated by the Holy Spirit and baptized with the Holy Spirit can ask and seek more of Him, creating more room for Him, evil will run as we demonstrate the power of sonship for good. I see that we are empowered to solve the problem of evil in this world. There is a good gift God wants to give the world to deal with the problem of evil—He is the Holy Spirit. Can the body of Christ rise to ask for more of the Holy Spirit to receive on behalf of all creation the good gift with power from on high? Rise, sons, and ask for more of the Holy Spirit.

As the manifestation of the Spirit becomes pervasive and prevalent through the body of Christ, the world will see the manifestation of the sons of God and people will be delivered from the bondage that they have been subjected to like all of creation. The time for all creation and creatures to be released from all bondage of evil is coming and is already here! The Holy Spirit manifests His fruits (Galatians 5:22–23) and charisma (1 Corinthians 12:7–11) through the body of Christ. As the gifts of the Son (Ephesians 4:7–16) equip the believers, making us more like the Son, Jesus, sharpened for effective witnessing of the power of the Holy Spirit in the world, we will reveal the goodness of God to the world. Evilness will be reduced anywhere and everywhere and eliminated in the dispensation of the fullness of time when the sons of God are fully revealed:

> 1 Corinthians 12:7, 11 (ESV)—"To each is given **the manifestation of the Spirit** for the common good...All these are empowered by **one and the same Spirit**, who apportions to each one individually as he wills.

Transformed by the Holy Spirit

In Galatians 5:22–23 (ESV), we read, "But the fruit of the Spirit is love, joy, peace, patience, kindness, goodness, faithfulness, gentleness, self-control; against such things, there is no law."

God the Father and the Son are giving something good to the world. He is the Holy Spirit manifesting through the body of Christ. Galatians 5:19–21 shows us behaviors that we know are evil—they are the result of human nature (self-life), the iniquity that dwells in us all:

> **Now the works of the flesh are evident: sexual immorality, impurity, sensuality, idolatry, sorcery, enmity, strife, jealousy, fits of anger, rivalries, dissensions, divisions, envy, drunkenness, orgies, and things like these. I warn you, as I warned you before, that those who do such things will not inherit the kingdom of God.** (ESV)

On the contrary, Galatians 5:22–23 shows us good virtues. We see here that the good that the world is looking for is the fruit of the third person of the Godhead, the Holy Spirit. So when we say that Jesus had given the ministry of good to the church, we are not talking about the building, but the Spirit-filled people regenerated by the Spirit, walking in the Spirit, and living by the Spirit. Those are the ones whose lives manifest God's good since they are the sons of God: "For all who are led by the Spirit of God are sons of God" (Romans 8:14 ESV).

A further read of Romans 8 shows us that creation is in bondage to evil and waiting for sons to manifest. And these sons are the agents of good and the eradicators of evil. They are those whom the Holy Spirit leads:

> For the Creation waits with eager longing for the **revealing of the sons of God**…that the Creation itself will be set free from its bondage to corruption and

obtain the freedom of the **glory of the children of God**. (Romans 8:19, 21 ESV)

So when you take verse 14 and verse 19–21 together, we could say that *creation waits with eager longing for the revelation of all whom the Spirit of God leads—those people are the sons of God.*

Therefore, the Holy Spirit is the essential embodiment of God's goodness in Christ, now manifested in and through the church. God does good and gives good gifts of the Holy Spirit. God has commissioned the church to be the carrier of His goodness to the world.

Whenever there is pain and agony, murder, discrimination, suffering, poverty, sicknesses, demon possession, oppression, and all manner of evil, it is a call for sons of God to arise. From what we're learning, who is the one that God has put in this world to show His goodness to a world under the bondage of evil? You might say the Holy Spirit, but the Holy Spirit needs a human body on the earth—like Jesus of Nazareth—just like the demons need bodies to operate on the earth.

Therefore, when we ask who the solution and response and the answer to the problem of evil to show God's goodness in the world is, it is you and I—regenerated, in communion with, filled, baptized with, and led by the Holy Spirit.

So Romans 12 gives us another dimension of the operation of the Holy Spirit in the body of Christ (sons of God) to spread God's goodness in the world. Listed in those verses of the Bible are virtues that the sons of God demonstrate to spread God's goodness in the world, proving that God is good and that He actively does what is good from the creation of the universe for all eternity.

Are you going through pain, sickness, suffering, sorrow, disaster, and death? You know where to go for the situation to be changed here and now. Go to the sons of God, go the body of Christ to receive good by the Holy Spirit in the body of Christ. There is power in the mighty name of Jesus by the finger of God, the Holy Spirit, to break every chain. Your time is now. Believe in God and see His hands work on your behalf. You will see for yourself that indeed God exists, and He is good.

I will end this chapter by going back to that scripture that Jesus gave in John 20:21–22 (ESV):

> Jesus said to them again, "Peace be with you. *As the Father has sent me, even so I am sending you.*" And when he had said this, he breathed on them and said to them, "Receive the Holy Spirit."

Do you want to experience the good gift of God, the Holy Spirit through regeneration—being born again from death to life by the Holy Spirit. I am praying that a new desire, passion, and need for the indwelling Holy Spirit will fill you. Such desire is the driving force for the good that God wants in a man. I pray that you will have the courage to find a private place where you can bow your head, fall on your face, bend your knees, or stand with arms spread wide and hearts open to ask for the Holy Spirit.

Perhaps you need to be filled and baptized with the Holy Spirit. If you are such a person, find a private place where you can pray and ask the Father to give you the Holy Spirit. Ask the Father for the freshness of the Holy Spirit, fresh infilling, and fresh baptism of the Holy Spirit so that you might be one of God's instruments of good in this world. In case you don't know how to do this, find a church that believes in the Bible and the Holy Spirit. Ask their leader or any member of that local assembly to guide you. You can also reach out to me.

Chapter Ten

God's Delegated Authority

Restraining Evil through Earthly Institutions

Apart from the body of Christ—a community of God's sons—where God's supernatural power and earthly governmental authority are delegated, God also has His authority delegated to established human institutions. The concept of delegated authorities and their place in God's plan to advance good and minimize evil are the focus of Romans 13:1–7.

> Let every person be subject to the governing authorities. For there is no authority except from God, and those that exist have been instituted by God. Therefore whoever resists the authorities resists what God has appointed, and those who resist will incur judgment. For rulers are not a terror to good conduct, but to bad. Would you have no fear of the one who is in authority? Then do what is good, and you will receive his approval, for he is God's servant for your good. But if you do wrong, be afraid, for he does not bear the sword in vain. For he is the servant of God, an avenger who carries out God's wrath on the wrongdoer. Therefore one must be in subjection, not only to avoid God's wrath but also for the sake of conscience. For because of this you also pay taxes, for the authorities are ministers of God, attending to this very thing. Pay to all what is owed to them: taxes to whom taxes are owed, revenue to whom revenue is owed,

respect to whom respect is owed, honor to whom honor is owed.

In chapter nine, it was communicated that as Jesus went about doing good and healing those oppressed by the Devil, the church is commissioned to do the same. We read in Romans 12 a list of some of the good deeds that the church is called to spread to let the world see that God is good. The church is God's human agent of good on the earth. In Romans 12:9 and Ephesians 2:10, God calls the body of Christ to do *only* what is good:

> Romans 12:9 (ESV)—"Your love must be real. Hate what is evil. **Do only what is good**."

> Ephesians 2:10 (TPT)—"We have become his poetry, a re-created people that will fulfill the destiny he has given each of us, for we are joined to Jesus, the Anointed One. Even before we were born, God planned in advance our destiny and **the good works we would do to fulfill it!**"

> Romans 12:21 (TPT)—"Never let evil defeat you, **but defeat evil with good**."

In Romans 12:21, the body of Christ is also called to fight evil by overcoming evil with good. In chapter 9, we saw that the church—filled and baptized with the Holy Spirit—is God's powerful instrument to promote His goodness and eradicate evil in the world.

The focus of this chapter is the concept of earthly delegated authority. Delegated authority is an authority you obtained from another person who has authority. Authority is delegated when they are constituted by the appropriate body with legal authority. So another way to talk about this delegated authority is constituted authority.

God's Power and His Human System of Delegated Authority

God established a system of authority and government in the world to show that He is good and only wants good to prevail. God doesn't want evil to succeed in the world. The system of authority or governance that God instituted in the world is like that given to the church, except that the church also has supernatural authority.

The overall purpose of these systems of authority is to do good and spread good in the world. The authority is delegated because it was given by God, who alone is authority. Just like God alone is good, He alone is Authority. According to the testimony of scripture, there is nobody or no entity in the world that holds essential authority but God Himself. God alone is the authority because power belongs to God alone: "Once God has spoken; twice have I heard this: that power belongs to God" (Psalm 62:11 ESV).

Power belongs to God, and because power belongs to God, authority is vested in this power. Everyone who has power received and derived it from God—even the Devil's power was the power he had as God's anointed cherub Lucifer and therefore derived from God. Again, power belongs to God. If anybody has power, it is because God has given it to them: **"For there is no authority except from God, and those that exist have been instituted by God"** (Romans 13:1 ESV).

Isaiah 40 also confirms that God does delegate power or authority to people: **"He gives power** to the faint, and to him who has no might he increases strength" (Isaiah 40:29 ESV).

We read in the previous chapter that Jesus said, "Behold, **I have given you authority** to tread on serpents and scorpions, and over all the power of the enemy, and nothing shall hurt you" (Luke 10:19 ESV).

All authority rests on God-given power, which brings about delegated authority.

Let us engage in a little exposition of Romans 13 to understand this concept of constituted or delegated authority: "Say, let every person be subject to the governing authorities. For there is no authority except from God. **And those that exist have been instituted by God (**Romans 13:1 ESV).

So another word that we could use for delegated authority is *instituted authority*. There is a system of authority on the earth that derives from God's power, whereby He controls the universe. This system of authority is called constituted, instituted, or delegated authority.

Merriam Webster dictionary defines "authority" as the power to give orders or decide, the power or right to direct or control someone or something. Therefore, according to the scripture, every instituted authority represents God. When a person or organization sets a system that gives power or right to give orders, decide, or enforce obedience (even political or administratively), such a system represents God and God's orderliness.

It might be difficult to accept that all authority represents God because some men in authority have perpetrated and perpetuated evil in the world. You would notice from the book of Romans 13 that God did not delegate authority with the intention that men would use it for evil purposes. Authority is given to do good and promote goodness. The same was true when God anointed Lucifer; He did not intend His authority to be used to perpetrate evil but to worship Him and promote His good purpose. I believe that with the fall of Lucifer, God knew that the world would need a system in place to encourage good and condemn evil while working His plans to mature in the fullness of time. Therefore, He instituted a system of authority in the world. Jude 1:6 supports this belief: "And the angels who did not stay within their own position of authority, but left their proper dwelling, he has kept in eternal chains under gloomy darkness until the judgment of the great day."

The Bible commands us to submit to the governing authority, institutional authority, or delegated authorities:

"Jesus said to them, 'Render to Caesar the things that are Caesar's, and to God the things that are God's.' And they marveled at him" (Mark 12:17 ESV).

To resist a system of authority is to oppose God's ordination—and there are consequences: "Therefore whoever resists the authorities resists what God has appointed, and those who resist will incur judgment" (Romans 13:2 ESV).

God instituted authorities in the world to avenge evil and to promote and encourage good since He is good and only does good. Delegated authorities are servants of God in this respect. They are to approve what is good and disapprove of evil. Whenever evil is done, they have a system of judgment in place, represented by a sword in Romans 13, to bring wrath upon the perpetrators of evil. Such judgment will manifest in the form of discipline, fines, time-out, detentions, spankings, or jail terms. All of these are God's ways to ensure evil is quickly punished so that the heart of men will not find it easy to perpetrate evil: "Because the sentence against an evil deed is not executed speedily, the heart of the children of man is fully set to do evil" (Ecclesiastes 8:11 ESV).

Romans 12:19–21 (ESV) tells individuals not to avenge evil but to overcome evil with good deeds:

> **Beloved, never avenge yourselves**, but leave it to the wrath of God, for it is written, "Vengeance is mine, I will repay, says the Lord." To the contrary, if your enemy is hungry, feed him; if he is thirsty, give him something to drink; for by so doing you will heap burning coals on his head. Do not be overcome by evil, **but overcome evil with good.**

However, God expects and demands that His delegated authority should repay evil and show vengeance against evil as the representative of God to whom vengeance belongs.

In essence, God wants humans, who will be sons of God, to experience good and promote goodness. Human beings should not avenge or repay evil with evil. However, He wants discipline to be executed on those who practice wickedness and rebel against delegated authority—those trying to corner the system and take advantage of the system to do evil.

There are examples of delegated authorities everywhere around you, from the home to the school system, local church, counties, cities, state government, and countries.

Delegated Authorities on the Earth

God gave parents the authority in the home to lead their children in the right way and ensure things are done in orderliness. God wants parent to raise godly offspring:

> Did he not make them one, with a portion of the Spirit in their union? *And what was the one God seeking? Godly offspring.* So guard yourselves in your spirit, and let none of you be faithless to the wife of your youth. (Malachi 2:15 ESV)

In workplaces, there are regulations, policies, laws, and bylaws with people empowered to enforce them to ensure things are done correctly, following good living and virtues. Teachers, principals, professors, vice-chancellors, presidents of institutions, leaders of organizations, etc., are appointed as delegated authority. And according to Romans 13, the authority has been given to them to approve of good and disapprove of evil. Government law enforcement agencies such as the police force have authority within their jurisdiction. They are to protect good people and punish bad people. They arrest criminals or violators of laws and order, charge them appropriately, and make them face the proper consequences proportional to the evils they have done in the community, county, state, or country.

For example, in America and other democratic systems of government, there are three arms of the systems of

188

government with instituted or constituted authorities derived from God, who combines all three in one as shown in Isaiah 33:22 (ESV): "For the LORD is our judge [judicial]; the LORD is our lawgiver [legislative]; the LORD is our king [executive]; he will save us."

Each arm of the government has power and jurisdiction. The judicial component interprets, defends, and applies the law to promote good and judge evil, usually in a court. The legislative makes laws that promote good deeds and curb evil. The executive administers the rules and enforces law and order. All three arms of government uphold good and disapprove of evil. They are to reward good and disdain and discipline evil within their jurisdiction. So anywhere you see authority constituted by law, policy, or bylaws, Romans 13:1 says it is to promote good in the world; we must subject ourselves to those governing authority.

We are to maintain an attitude of reverence for constituted authority. We are to obey constituted authority. That is one of God's ways of ensuring the advancement of goodness globally. Of course, you may have examples of situations where authorities have perpetrated evil. Unfortunately, those are corrupted authorities like Satan. The proper way to stop such corrupted people is to use a higher delegated or human authority to disapprove and discipline them so that we can promote good in keeping with the purpose of delegated authority.

Those in whom the Holy Spirit resides and those who understand the purpose of constituted, instituted, appointed, or delegated authority should seek to occupy the seat of authority. Such people stand a higher chance of properly using the delegated authority. Know that the purpose of authority is not to promote self. It is not to enrich self. It is intended to ensure that good is promoted and evil is disapproved.

As ministers of God, everyone in the place of authority will be judged by God as stewards of that authority. Authorities are God's instrument to promote what is suitable for a peaceful and orderly life on the earth. Therefore, it seems fitting that

189

God's children should see it as a responsibility to seek opportunities to serve humanity and the purpose of God through appointment and election into the places of authority. In that way, the church can invade spheres of society as God's agents of good in this world while we wait for the culmination of all things.

Let God's sons find their way to the seat of authorities and governments in the world as stewards of God's authority. The earnest expectation of creation is waiting for the manifestation of the sons of God. A time is coming when the kingdom of this world will become the kingdom of our God and His Christ: "Then the seventh angel blew his trumpet, and there were loud voices in heaven, saying, 'The kingdom of the world has become the kingdom of our Lord and of his Christ, and he shall reign forever and ever'" (Revelation 11:15 ESV).

Why not let those of us who are sons and daughters of God hold the fort in our different localities and spheres while we wait for the completion of all things? The time is coming, and now is when the kingdoms of this world shall become the kingdom of God.

Read what scripture has to say about authority in the home:

> Children, obey your parents in the Lord, for this is right. "Honor your father and mother" (this is the first commandment with a promise), that it may go well with you and that you may live long in the land. Fathers, do not provoke your children to anger, but bring them up in the discipline and instruction of the Lord. (Ephesians 6:1–4 ESV)

See also Ephesians 5:22 (KJV): "Wives, submit yourselves unto your husband, as unto the Lord."

In schools, students are subject to the authority of their teachers and their principals, and we are called to follow the laws, policies, and bylaws at the workplace. We are to submit to our leaders as long as they stay within the constituted rules, policies, and bylaws. We are to honor those in authority. We are to respect them.

Mayors and governors have delegated authorities. The judge in the law court is another person operating in an office with instituted authority. A correct judge weights all options of an accused person within the bounds of the law with a clear conscience and decides on the appropriate sentence commensurate with what they have done. The judge is expected to convict a criminal to keep evil at bay in his locality. In other words, judges are expected to be just. In reality, the judge is only operating on the delegated authority vested in him by the land's law. His/her authority is ultimately derived from God's absolute power, the judge of all the earth.

> Genesis 18:25 (ESV)—"Far be it from you to do such a thing, to put the righteous to death with the wicked, so that the righteous fare as the wicked! Far be that from you! **Shall not the Judge of all the earth do what is just?**"

> Psalm 94:1–2 (ESV)—"O LORD, God of vengeance, O God of vengeance, shine forth! Rise up, **O Judge of the earth**; repay to the proud what they deserve!"

God is the judge of all the earth. Whenever any person in the office operating under instituted authority is unjust and promoting evil, the children can file allegations or sue such a one in the highest court of the earth in the place of prayer— the court of heaven where God is the judge. And we can rest assured that God, the judge of all the earth, will do what is right. The way to approach God to vindicate you or judge over a situation is to pray. Legislators are required to make laws that are fair and free of discrimination according to just standards and ensure they pass such regulations into laws in good conscience so that the judicial arm of the government will make sure things are done in orderliness and *to promote good and to disapprove of evil.* And then the executive arm of the government—kings or presidents—ensure the use of their executive authorities to promote good things for all people in the land who operate within the law.

According to Romans 13:4, all these authorities are delegated and are the servants of God for good. So corrupted men in the place of authorities, who promote evil, will be judged by the highest authority, God—the Judge of the earth! *If you are operating in an office endowed with delegated authority, you must do it with fear, trembling, and a clear conscience. You must be sure that you are promoting good—otherwise, you are misrepresenting God.* Beware because you are a minister of God handling the authority that belongs to God. God intends to use His power to advance good behavior on the earth to reveal His goodness. You are a steward of God's delegated authority. I believe that if delegated authority operates justly and fairly, we will gradually have fewer questions from people about the goodness of God because they would have seen God's just, fair, and good nature in people operating with delegated authority.

At the beginning of this book, my premise was that God alone is good, and here we are saying God alone is authority. So there is no authority anywhere but God. Therefore, delegated authority is for the advancement of God's good purpose. When instituted authorities promote evil behavior, it is an abuse of authority, which puts the violator under the judgment of God, who is Authority Himself.

The Authority of God's Son in Prayer over Delegated Authorities

I will connect this chapter to some portion of chapter 9. In that chapter, I said that the church is God's agent to destroy the Devil's works and promote good in the world. One of the main ways the church enforces good and judges evil on the earth is through prayer.

There are different categories of prayers. 1 Timothy 2:1–4 gives examples of the type of prayer that the church should engage in:

> First of all, then, I urge that **supplications**, **prayers**, **intercessions**, and **thanksgivings** be made for all people, for kings and all who are in high positions, that we may lead a peaceful and quiet life, godly and dignified in every way. This is good, and it is pleasing in the sight of God our Savior, who desires all people to be saved and to come to the knowledge of the truth. (ESV)

The church is the primary place where God put authority and can exert that authority from the spiritual dimension through the ministry of prayer. In the place of prayer, the church has authority given to us by Jesus. Prayer is so powerful to move the hearts of men having delegated authority such as kings to ensure good is effectuated on the earth. The power of prayer to turn leaders' hearts in the direction of good is confirmed in Proverbs 21:1: "The King's heart is a stream of water in the hand of the LORD; he turns it wherever he will."

According to 1 Timothy 2:1–4, the church should pray for people in authority because we can direct the heart of men in authority towards God's good purpose through prayer.

So the sons of God should understand that we are God's instrument on the earth to move the heart of every leader. We have spiritual and supernatural authority. By prayer, we can move the heart of every king, every mayor, every governor, every president, every judge, every father, every mother, every teacher, every boss, and people in a high positions in the direction of God's good purpose. We are to pray, make supplication, intercede, and give thanks on their behalf so that men can lead a peaceful and quiet life and are dignified in every way. Basically, **"this is good"** (1 Timothy 2:3)—this is how you promote good in the world. Praying and interceding to promote good is pleasing in the sight of God, our Savior, who desires all people to be saved and come to the knowledge of the truth.

Let us Pray:

> Oh God, give us the spirit of prayer. Dear Lord, raise intercessors who can move the heart of leaders to favor good deeds with their authority so that the whole world may know and share in the goodness of God in the land of the living.

Imagine what the world would look like if all authorities and people in a position of authority stood for doing good with no corruption of power to do evil.

An illustration to help us understand the power of prayer for promoting good in the world is the story of Nehemiah. Nehemiah understood that it was a good cause to build the broken wall of Israel:

> The words of Nehemiah the son of Hacaliah. Now it happened in the month of Chislev, in the twentieth year, as I was in Susa the citadel, that Hanani, one of my brothers, came with certain men from Judah. And I asked them concerning the Jews who escaped, who had survived the exile, and concerning Jerusalem. **And they said to me, "The remnant there in the province who had survived the exile is in great trouble and shame. The wall of Jerusalem is broken down, and its gates are destroyed by fire." As soon as I heard these words I sat down and wept and mourned for days, and I continued fasting and praying before the God of heaven.** (Nehemiah 1:1–4 ESV)

After understanding this, in Nehemiah 1:4, Nehemiah fasted and prayed to God. Prayers like this illustrate the prayer ministry of the church in the world. But in the context of this chapter, it is a prayer to move the heart of people in authority to advance God's good cause on the earth.

When referring to a case of demon possession, Jesus said, "However, this kind does not go out except by prayer and fasting" (Matthew 17:21 NKJV).

For example, let's say we have a king possessed by demons and who therefore began to perpetrate and perpetuate evil; Jesus said in the scripture that this kind of demon wouldn't go out except by fasting and prayer. So it seems to me that when you have leaders oppressed or possessed by the Devil, thereby promoting evil instead of good like Saul, we need to engage their hearts by prayer and fasting and thanksgiving like David did with King Saul of Israel: "And whenever the harmful spirit from God was upon Saul, David took the lyre and played it with his hand. So, Saul was refreshed and was well, and the harmful spirit departed from him" (1 Samuel 16:23 ESV).

Notice that the statement "harmful spirit from God" makes it look as if God directly sent a harmful spirit to Saul. A proper understanding of statements like this was addressed in chapter 2 of the book. It simply means God allowed it as He did with Job.

As the church, we must learn to pray for our leaders because "**this is** how we promote **good**" (1 Timothy 2:3). Some of the unsaved men in authority might already be a captive of the Devil themselves. Nehemiah fasted and prayed to move the heart of the king in the direction of God's good cause to build the broken wall of Israel in Nehemiah 2:1–8 (ESV):

> In the month of Nisan, in the twentieth year of King Artaxerxes, when wine was before him, I took up the wine and gave it to the King. Now I had not been sad in his presence. And the King said to me, "Why is your face sad, seeing you are not sick? This is nothing but sadness of the heart." Then I was very much afraid. I said to the king, "Let the King live forever! Why should not my face be sad, when the city, the place of my fathers' graves, lies in ruins, and its gates have been destroyed by fire?" Then

the King said to me, "What are you requesting?" So I prayed to the God of heaven. And I said to the King, "If it pleases the king, and if your servant has found favor in your sight, that you send me to Judah, to the city of my fathers' graves, that I may rebuild it." And the King said to me (the queen sitting beside him), "How long will you be gone, and when will you return?" So it pleased the King to send me when I had given him a time. And I said to the King, "If it pleases the King, let letters be given me to the governors of the province beyond the River, that they may let me pass through until I come to Judah, and a letter to Asaph, the keeper of the King's forest, that he may give me timber to make beams for the gates of the fortress of the temple, and for the wall of the city, and for the house that I shall occupy." **And the King granted me what I asked, for the good hand of my God was upon me.**

When Nehemiah prayed to promote God's good cause, the "good hand of the Lord rested on him." The hand that moves the world began to move things in the direction of Nehemiah because Nehemiah aligned with the purpose of God; therefore, the power of God moved the king's heart. I believe if we want to see the good hand of the Lord working on the earth for good, we need to identify and align with His purpose on the earth, fast and pray for him to move the heart of leaders to do His will; then we will see the glory of the Lord in the land of the living.

My heart's desire and prayers as you're reading is that the good hand of the Lord God will be upon you right now, and you will go on your knees and pray for all the authorities that you know that God will move their heart to promote a good cause in the world.

Pray for men with delegated authority in your home, school, church, city council, county, state, and country. Even if you have an evil leader that is frustrating a good cause of God, you can persevere in prayer and fasting until God changes their heart to favor you as the good hand of the Lord

196

comes upon you. Even an unjust judge's heart can be changed through faith and perseverance in prayer as found in Luke 18:1–8 (ESV):

> And he told them a parable to the effect that **they ought always to pray and not lose heart.** He said, "In a certain city there was a judge who neither feared God nor respected man. And there was a widow in that city who kept coming to him and saying, 'Give me justice against my adversary.' For a while he refused, but afterward he said to himself, **'Though I neither fear God nor respect man, yet because this widow keeps bothering me, I will give her justice, so that she will not beat me down by her continual coming.'"** And the Lord said, "Hear what the unrighteous judge says. And will not God give justice to his elect, who cry to him day and night? Will he delay long over them? I tell you, he will give justice to them speedily. **Nevertheless, when the Son of Man comes, will he find faith on Earth?"**

The whole point of this chapter is to make you see that God could not be evil. And God must be good because the authorities set in place in the world and representing Him are testament or witness to His good nature. God has a plan to deal with evil in time and ultimately at the end of time. God will eradicate corruption in the world at the fullness of time.

I have heard people question the goodness of God when the Bible writes stories of God judging a people or city in the Old Testament. How can He be good when He committed genocide against an entire nation? They accuse God of ethnic cleansing. Upon first looking from a western perspective, I must admit that it appears that we cannot justify God's action. However, upon second look, if God is the judge of all the earth and is omniscient, then He knows all situations surrounding the people He decided to wipe out that we may not know.

If earthly judges with delegated authority are considered good when they judge a criminal, say a serial killer, in the court based on their knowledge of the law of that locality, then God, who has all knowledge by which He judges, must be good. So it would not be fair and nearly blasphemous to call a mere human judge good when they judge and then call God evil when He judges in His realm. Are the policemen evil when they arrest a criminal because they know by the law of the land that that person is a criminal? Could it be possible that if we see into the mind of God, some of those judgments that we've read about in scriptures and in history that make us question the benevolence of God will make sense? Just like we will be saying a police officer by arresting somebody evil and criminal is doing good, God is also doing good when He judges evil.

Here is what the Bible said when God was Judging the famous Sodom and Gomorrah: "Far be it from you to do such a thing, to put the righteous to death with the wicked, so that the righteous fare as the wicked! Far be that from you! **Shall not the Judge of all the earth do what is just?**" (Genesis 18:25 ESV).

Do you have some form of authority conferred on you, either by appointment or through the government? Remember, you are one of those ministers to make sure the world does not ever question the goodness of God. You must make sure that evil does not have a field day and that good is rewarded and promoted. Ensure that men can see through your just and exemplary leadership that God is good and will ultimately eradicate evil from existence although evil is currently present. Will you rise to this commission from God? Will you use your authority, given by God, to promote God's good purpose?

I call you also to stand up to represent God well by your seat of delegated authority. You might wonder where to start. Start with that woman and her child who needs your support to get what is due to them. Avenge her of her adversaries. Don't be like an unjust judge in the scripture in

Luke 18:1–8. So rise to your commission, submit to the authority of God, submit to the governing authority, and exercise delegated authority to advance God's good cause in the world. The good hand of the Lord will rest on you, and men will see that God is good through your ministry as God works all things together for good.

SECTION 4

HOPE WHILE MAKING SENSE OF THE PROBLEM OF EVIL

Chapter Eleven

Answering Typical Questions During Pain and Suffering

Why Does God Allow Pain and Suffering?

In this chapter, I speak to some of the typical questions that people ask during pain and suffering. Evil matters because it causes people pain, sorrow, suffering, and death. I argue that nobody would care about its existence if what we call evil did not result in pain, sorrow, suffering, and death. When we go through a very tough time, illness, or other unpalatable situation, we may ask interesting questions that come close to doubting the goodness of God. They are questions that cast aspersion on the integrity of God. Examples of such questions include "Why do bad things happen to good people?" and "Where was God when this evil was happening?" These kinds of questions are legitimate questions that any honest, rational, and genuine person would ask in light of the benevolence of God and His omnipotence, omnipresence, and omniscience.

In my attempt to respond to these questions, I would first like to remind you about chapter 5, where we talked about the origin of the perpetration of evil. In that chapter, we concluded that the Devil is the "doer" of **evil,** which he does through his demon (evil spirits) and human selfish desires. In a nutshell, if anyone is experiencing any form of evil, it is primarily the work of the Devil and the wickedness of the unregenerated human heart filled with iniquity. We live in a fallen universe. Romans 8:18-30 confirms that the bondage we see in creation is because creation has been subjected to captivity by the Devil. In other words, evil has been intertwined in the fabric of nature since the rebellion of angels and the fall of man.

One way to illustrate the coexistence of evil and good now is the parable of the wheat and weed in Matthew 13:23–30 (ESV):

> He put another parable before them, saying, "The kingdom of heaven may be compared to a man who sowed **good seed [God's good creation]** in his field, **but while his men were sleeping,** his **enemy came and sowed weeds among the wheat [rebellion of angels and fall of man]** and went away. So when the plants came up and bore grain, **then the weeds appeared also.** And the servants of the master of the house came and said to him, 'Master, **did you not sow good seed in your field?** How **then does it have weeds?' [The question people ask—where was God? How do bad things happen to good people?]** He said to them, '**An enemy has done this**.' So the servants said to him, 'Then do you want us to go and gather them?' But he said, 'No, **lest in gathering the weeds you root up the wheat along with them.' Let both grow together until the Harvest**, and at harvest time I will tell the reapers, 'Gather the weeds first and bind them in bundles to be burned **[The lake of fire created for the Devil and his angels]**, but gather the wheat into my barn.'"

The weeds and the wheat must grow together until the time of harvest. The weeds represent the growth of evil, and the wheat represents the growth and spread of good. And it seems that trying to root out all the weeds before the fullness of time when God will sort things out very clearly may result in rooting out wheat as well. This plan makes sense because some situations have resulted in an unfair judgment of good people. After all, the human perception of good is limited. Only God has the complete knowledge to determine what aligns with goodness. However, God wants a maximum harvest of sons in this world, so He will not judge all the evil before the time for harvest.

In chapter 6, I discussed God's eternal purpose and desire. Romans 8:28 demonstrates that God's purpose is to make sons of God out of sons of men. This is the wheat harvest parable. As shown in chapter 5, God created Adam and Eve (good seed). Adam and Eve fell in the garden of Eden (weed sown by the enemy), and the principle of evil is now part of the DNA of man and part of the fabric of creation. No wonder the Bible said in Genesis 6:5–6 (ESV) that the imagination of the heart of a man is now evil continuously: "The LORD saw that the wickedness of man was great in the earth, and that **every intention of the thoughts of his heart was only *evil* continually.** And the LORD regretted that he had made man on the earth, and it grieved him to his heart." (ESV)

So the entire creation is now infected with the "weed" called iniquity, which is a principle of evil. The whole creation is in pain, bondage, and agony. Therefore, whenever we see evil, pain, and suffering in any part of humanity (a subset of all creation), it is a manifestation of the weed called iniquity sown by the Devil. Unfortunately, weeds grow naturally, and nothing can stop them except someone intervenes. That person must be the servants (ministers) of God. In God's own time, He will supernaturally, without the need for any man, get rid of the weeds at the end of times—the harvest. However, in a measure, His servants who want to minimize evil in time will have to do it carefully by stepping into the situations under His help.

Essentially, bad things happen to good people because evil is currently part of the fabric of creation, and unregenerated humans are agents of evil like demons and the Devil. Where was God when evil was happening in time? He has been on His throne, counting on His servants (ministers) to stand up and prevent evil from happening. We have discussed God's ministers in the world in chapters 9 and 10—the body of Christ (God's children) and earthly human delegated authority. These servants do not have all things figured out as He does, so they must be careful in doing this, staying under His leadership lest they root out the wheat as well—lest they destroy sons in the process. Simply put, when evil is being perpetrated and God seems silent, it is because God has stewarded His good works to His agents in the world—primarily the sons of God (the church) and secondarily His human delegated authorities. Psalm 115:16 shows that God has stewarded the earth to man: "The heavens are the LORD's heavens, but the earth he has given to the children of man." (ESV)

That explains why God will be very strict when He judges men who are believers for a reward at the Bema throne of Jesus Christ. The Bema throne is the title given to the judgment seat of Christ where believers will give an account of their lives to Christ for eternal reward (2 Corinthians 5:10, Romans 14:10). Just like the Devil uses humans as the agent of evil, you and I could be the agents of good to demonstrate His goodness in the world. Someone is waiting for you; some situation is waiting for you to root out weeds.

When God wraps things up, the glory of creation will be revealed, and there will be no more evil. Why does He not do it now? He wants sons from the earth; He wants maximum harvest slated for the time of harvest. Until then, God leads men by His Spirit through the prayer of the sons of God and by His system of delegated authority to stop evil in any locality and any person's life:

> Act 1:7–8 (ESV)—"He said to them, **"It is not for you to know times or seasons that the Father has fixed by his own authority. But you will receive power when the Holy Spirit has come upon** you, **and you will be my witnesses** in Jerusalem and in all Judea and Samaria, and to the end of the earth."

Knowing God will eradicate evil someday and manifest the fullness of sonship, consider that the sufferings of this present time are not worth comparing with the glory that is to be revealed to us: "For I consider that the sufferings of this present time are not worth comparing with the glory that is to be revealed to us" (Romans 8:18 ESV).

The scripture above clearly tells us that the Bible does acknowledge the fact that there is suffering in this present time. Such acknowledgment should immediately make you pause and think about how reliable the scripture is as a source of consolation, a source of change, and a source of hope in the time of suffering or pain that you might be going through. The Bible does not pretend like suffering is distant from nature. Therefore, it should be considered a trustworthy guide toward the solution to the problem of evil.

To eliminate potential confusion, let me say right off the bat that every time you see the pain and suffering, it is the work of the Devil. God allowed it, based on His infinite knowledge and wisdom, because He has judged that He could work that situation together for good. God never has and will never willingly author act of evil toward anyone. Still, He may allow it temporarily for His ultimate good purpose, which is to reveal sons and conform us in growth more to the image of His Son. Therefore, creation was subjected to futility, not willingly, but because of Him who subjected it in hope. *I believe the suffering in creation leads to the birth or harvest of God's sons everywhere and at every time. The problem is that we do not have the big picture in all situations and circumstances to see it. Think about it.*

Why Do Bad Things Happen to Good People?

The question is often asked during pain and suffering: "Why do bad things happen to good people?" It is because there is a Devil and his demons who have sown the seed of evil in the fabric of creation and the heart of humans. But God cannot eradicate evil men because He needs them to grow His wheat

206

(sons). You might call this the "God dilemma." The Devil sowed what God does not want in what God needed for His purpose. And God's plan to separate both without losing the baby with the bathwater must be done in time and by His well-trained agents (ministers). Unfortunately, because the ministers themselves can be corrupted by iniquity, they can also sometimes become an agent of evil to good people. Finally, as clearly stated throughout this book, there are no "good" people. We only have people with evil hearts that God is working to make good—God alone is good:

> Mark 10:18 (NIV)—"'Why do you call me good?' Jesus answered. 'No one is good—**except** God alone.'"
> Genesis 6:5 (ESV)—"The LORD saw that the wickedness of man was great in the earth, and that **every intention of the thoughts of his heart was only evil continually.**"

> Romans 8:28 (ESV)—"And we know that **for those who love God all things work together for good,** for those who are called according to his purpose."

> Ephesians 1:11(ESV)—"In him we have obtained an inheritance, having been predestined according to **the purpose of him who works all things according to the counsel of his will.**"

The pain and suffering that we see are signs that the sons of God are being birthed and harvested. It is like a woman giving birth to a child. Like a mother in labor, the suffering pales in light of the precious beautiful baby that will be born. The labor pains of childbirth, which is a microcosm of the pain in all of creation, was the result of the fall, and therefore ultimately the work of the Devil. However, the birth of the baby is the work of God and the plan of God:

> There is no such thing as darkness with you. The night, to you, is as bright as the day; there's no difference

between the two. **You formed my innermost being, shaping my delicate inside and my intricate outside, and wove them all together in my mother's womb.** I thank you, God, for making me so mysteriously complex! Everything you do is marvelously breathtaking. It simply amazes me to think about it! How thoroughly you know me, Lord! You even formed every bone in my body when you created me in the secret place, carefully, skillfully shaping me from nothing to something. You saw who you created me to be before I became me! Before I'd ever seen the light of day, the number of days you planned for me were already recorded in your book. Every single moment you are thinking of me! How precious and wonderful to consider that you cherish me constantly in your every thought! **O God, your desires toward me are more than the grains of sand on every shore! When I awake each morning, you're still with me.** (Psalm 139:12–18 TPT)

According to these verses, God has put a message in childbirth for us to see how God's good purpose is being accomplished using the Devil's evil intention of pain and suffering. No wonder the Bible says,

1 Timothy 2:15 (TPT)—"Yet **a woman shall live in restored dignity by means of her children**."

1 Timothy 2:15 (ESV)—"Yet she will be saved through childbearing."

Genesis 3:15 (ESV)—"And I will put enmity between thee and the woman, and between thy seed and her seed; it shall bruise thy head, and thou shalt bruise his heel."

Why Blame God?

If you are a slave to iniquity, then you shouldn't blame God for your pain and suffering. A person living habitually in sin is a slave of sin and is a candidate for bondage. Only those whom the Son frees are free indeed. The whole world is under the power of the evil one; only the house of God is immune to evil. Only sons can abide in His house forever:

> "And ye shall know the truth, and the truth shall make you free." They answered him, "We be Abraham's seed, and were never in bondage to any man: how sayest thou, 'Ye shall be made free?'" Jesus answered them, "Verily, verily, I say unto you, whosoever committeth sin is the servant of sin. And **the servant abideth not in the house forever: but the son abideth ever.** If the Son, therefore, shall make you free, ye shall be free indeed." (John 8:32–36 KJV)

Isaiah 59 paints a very great picture of why some people experience evil and God seems silent. Why? You may be asking the question, "Where was God when this and that was happening to me?"

> **Behold, the LORD'S hand is not shortened, that it cannot save; neither his ear heavy, that it cannot hear: But your iniquities have separated between you and your God, and your sins have hid his face from you, that he will not hear.** (Isaiah 59:1–2 KJV)

Isaiah 59:1–2 makes it clear that God is so good that He wants to save. He wants to grab us by His hands and pull us into the secret place of His house where we will abide under His shadows (Psalm 91:1). He wants to hear our cry for salvation (Psalm 91:15–16) when we call on His name. He wants to keep us in His safe house where no evil can touch us.

> **He that dwelleth in the secret place of the Most High shall abide under the shadow of the Almighty...He shall call upon me, and I will answer him: I will be with him in trouble; I will deliver him, and honour**

him. With long life will I satisfy him, and shew him my salvation. (Psalm 91:1, 15–16 KJV)

However, according to Isaiah 59:2, He cannot save someone living in sin under the power of iniquity: "**The Lord knoweth how to deliver the godly out of temptations,** and to reserve the unjust unto the day of judgment to be punished." (2 Peter 2:9 KJV)

Isaiah 59:2–13 shows a clear list of evil that men under the power of iniquity do. Essentially, living under iniquity violates the just nature of a good God to prevent evil from happening to you. Maybe if one of His sons pray, there might be enough reasons for him to save you from evil. But in general, a person who is a slave to sin has "shortened" the hand and "deafened" the ear of the Lord. If you sow evil, you will reap evil. Isaiah 59:19–21 and Genesis 8:22 confirm this:

> Genesis 8:22 (ASV)—"While the earth remaineth, seedtime and harvest, and cold and heat, and summer and winter, and day and night shall not cease."

> Isaiah 59:19–21 (KJV)—"So shall they fear the name of the LORD from the west, and his glory from the rising of the sun. When the enemy shall come in like a flood, the Spirit of the LORD shall lift a standard against him. And the Redeemer shall come to Zion, and unto them that turn from transgression in Jacob, saith the LORD. As for me, this is my covenant with them, saith the LORD; My spirit that is upon thee, and my words which I have put in thy mouth, shall not depart out of thy mouth, nor out of the mouth of thy seed, nor out of the mouth of thy seed's seed, saith the LORD, from henceforth and forever."

Isaiah 59:19–21, however, shows that as soon as a person turns from transgression and evil and fears the name of the Lord—who is holy—God will raise a standard against the Devil on your behalf. So if you are experiencing evil in your life, do you want to take account of your life and deeds? Are you reaping the evil deeds you have sown and have not genuinely repented from? Is there a sin that you need to repent from so that the blood of Jesus might cover all of these sins? If you find one, come boldly to the throne of grace now by faith to obtain mercy from God.

> Hebrews 4:14–16 (KJV)—"Seeing then that we have a great high priest, that is passed into the heavens, Jesus the Son of God, let us hold fast our profession. **For we have not an high priest which cannot be touched with the feeling of our infirmities; but was in all points tempted like as we are, yet without sin. Let us, therefore, come boldly unto the throne of grace, that we may obtain mercy, and find grace to help in time of need.**

He is waiting for you. Come home, oh you sinner, from your wayward ways. Come home, oh you prodigal. The arm of the Father is wide open to forgive your sins and redeem you from your evil ways.

Luke 24:46–47 (KJV)—"And said unto them, Thus it is written, and thus it behoved Christ to suffer, and to rise from the dead the third day: And that **repentance and remission of sins** should be preached in his name among all nations, beginning at Jerusalem."

According to Luke 24:46–47, God calls you to repentance as a basis for your sins to be forgiven. Jesus will wipe away your sins according to Hebrews 8:12 (ESV), "For I will be merciful toward their iniquities, and I will remember their sins no more."

Regardless of how dark or red your sins are, Jesus will make you white as snow and wool today. Read Isaiah 1:18–20 (ESV):

> Come now, and let us reason together, saith the LORD: though your sins be as scarlet, they shall be as white as

211

snow; though they be red like crimson, they shall be as wool. If ye be willing and obedient, ye shall eat the good of the land. But if ye refuse and rebel, ye shall be devoured with the sword: for the mouth of the LORD hath spoken it.

It is people like you that Jesus came for:

But their scribes and Pharisees murmured against his disciples, saying, "Why do ye eat and drink with publicans and sinners?" And Jesus answering said unto them, "They that are whole need not a physician; but they that are sick. I came not to call the righteous, but sinners to repentance." (Luke 5:30–32 KJV)

From now on, ask for the grace to be willing and obedient to Him, and you will start to experience His goodness in the land of the living: "If ye be willing and obedient, ye shall eat the good of the land" (Isaiah 1:19 KJV).

What about the Innocent—Where Was God in Their Situation?

One perfect example by which I will address the issue of evil happening to innocent people is a story in John 9:1–38. Read the scripture before continuing.

This story is compelling. It addresses the very root of the problem of evil. If anyone could be considered good and innocent, it would be a child in the womb. Yet this child was born *blind*, and he remained blind till adulthood. In keeping with the last section, someone might argue that his woe is because of the sin of his parents—that his parents were just reaping the harvest of the evil they had sown. If that were the case, it would be worrisome that an unborn baby would reap the consequences of the parents' sin in light of Ezekiel 18:20. Ezekiel 18:20 nullifies Deuteronomy 5:9:

Ezekiel 18:20 (ESV)— The soul who sins shall die. **The son shall not suffer for the iniquity of the father, nor the father suffers for the iniquity of the son.** The righteousness of the righteous shall be upon himself, and the wickedness of the wicked shall be upon himself.

Deuteronomy 5:9 (ESV)—You shall not bow down to them or serve them; for I the LORD your God am a jealous God, **visiting the iniquity of the fathers on the children to the third and fourth generation of those who hate me**.

Without a doubt, Jesus made it clear that neither the parents' nor the child's sin resulted in his blindness from birth:

Jesus answered, 'It was not that this man sinned, or his parents, but that the works of God might be displayed in him'" (John 9:3 ESV).

Therefore, this is an obvious example of an innocent person suffering. I can relate to this very well. This story has served as a consolation for my wife and I as we watched our beloved Ayanfeoluwa Achsah Agboola suffer from the symptoms of a Chromosome 18-q deletion genetic anomaly.

In keeping with the thesis of this book, Jesus revealed that the suffering of this innocent soul is so that the work of God might be displayed. What is the work of God?

John 6:28–29, 40 (ESV)— Then they said to him, 'What must we do, to be doing the works of God?' Jesus answered them, '**This is the work of God, that you believe in him whom he has sent**...For this is the will of My Father, **that everyone who looks on the Son and believes in him should have eternal life,** and I will raise him up on the last day.

The work of God is to encourage belief in the Son so that men can become sons of God: "But as many as received

213

him, **to them gave the power to become the sons of God, even to them that believe on his name:** Which were born, not of blood, nor of the will of the flesh, nor of the will of man, but of God" (John 1:12 KJV).

To confirm this to be true in the life of the man that was born blind, let's see how the story ended:

> Jesus heard that they had cast him out, and having found him he said, "Do you believe in the Son of Man?" He answered, **"And who is he, sir, that I may believe in him?"** Jesus said to him, "You have seen him, and **it is he who is speaking to you."** He said, **"Lord, I believe," and he worshiped him**. (John 9:35–38 ESV)

I understood from this story why my daughter was born with Chromosome 18-q deletion. It is so that the work of God might be displayed—that men may believe in Jesus the Son of God and be saved to become sons of God. In my case, I understand that this book may be born to receive many sons to glory. What if the purpose of Ayanfeoluwa's existence is to get me to the point where I can write the book that you now read so that you and many more can believe in the Son of God and partake in the glory of the only begotten Son of God for all eternity? I judge very strongly that this is the case for my daughter. Her pain and suffering could be an expression of God's love to reveal His work and glorify His Son at some point in her life to harvest many sons to glory. I have looked at her repeatedly, and I could not understand the source of her joy. She does not seem to be living in sorrow, although I am often crushed by the thought of what she might be going through in her mind. Essentially, "out of the ashes of her dying and our dying," a new day is breaking forth. God is gaining her and many sons to glory—this looks so much like the principle that Jesus revealed through his death to me. Paul understood this when he said, "So death is at work in us, but life in you" (2 Corinthians 4:12 ESV).

What about Believers Who Suffer?

The Bible teaches that Christians do suffer and face tribulations, that the sons of God do suffer in this world: "I have said these things to you, that in me you may have peace. In the world, you will have tribulation. But take heart; I have overcome the world" (John 16:33 ESV).

A believer's suffering and tribulations are the persecution and perils they face as they seek to become agents of God's good purpose in the world. They face this suffering as part of the raging battle against evil in the world—not as doers of evil themselves. 1 Peter 4:12–16 clarifies that this suffering is a suffering that leads to glory. Romans 8:16–19 explains the suffering of heirs—sons of God—is preparation for the glory to be revealed. So if a believer is suffering, as long as it is not for evildoing, the Bible says we should rejoice in hope amid the suffering and pray for deliverance from it all (1 Peter 4:13, Romans 5:3, Romans 12:12). Psalm 34:19 (ESV)— "Many are the afflictions of the righteous, but the LORD delivers him out of them all."

We are commanded not to be ashamed of such suffering, the kind that was in the life of our brother Paul, the apostle, as clearly delineated in 2 Corinthians 1 to 12. The early apostles faced persecution by the Sanhedrin council in Jerusalem (Acts 4:1–6; 5:40). The kind that led to Stephen's death (Acts 7:54–8:1), the kind that led to James's death, and Peter's imprisonment (Acts 12:1–17), etc. Hebrews chapters 10 and 11 records these kinds of suffering that believers go through. Some relevant texts of scriptures are given as follows:

> Romans 12:12 (ESV)—"Rejoice in hope, be patient in tribulation, be constant in prayer."

> 1 Peter 4:12–16 (ESV)—"Beloved, do not be surprised at the fiery trial when it comes upon you to test you, as though something strange were happening to you. But rejoice insofar as you share Christ's sufferings, that you

215

may also rejoice and be glad when his glory is revealed. If you are insulted for the name of Christ, you are blessed, because the Spirit of glory and of God rests upon you. But let none of you suffer as a murderer or a thief or an evildoer or as a meddler. Yet if anyone suffers as a Christian, let him not be ashamed, but let him glorify God in that name."

Romans 8:16–19—"The Spirit himself bears witness with our spirit that we are children of God. And if children, then heirs—heirs of God and fellow heirs with Christ, provided we suffer with him in order that we may also be glorified with him. For I consider that the sufferings of this present time are not worth comparing with the glory that is to be revealed to us. For the creation waits with eager longing for the revealing of the sons of God."

Sometimes, people suffer evil, pain, suffering, and tribulations because they are righteous. People might hate you because you believe and have become a son of God—promoting good among an evil and adulterous generations. Jesus stated this clearly in Matthew 10:21–25 (ESV):

Brother will deliver brother over to death, and the father his child, and children will rise against parents and have them put to death, and you will be hated by all for my name's sake. But the one who endures to the end will be saved. When they persecute you in one town, flee to the next, for truly, I say to you, you will not have gone through all the towns of Israel before the Son of Man comes. A disciple is not above his teacher, nor a servant above his master. It is enough for the disciple to be like his teacher, and the servant like his master. If they have called the master of the house Beelzebul, how much more will they malign those of his household.

Every society has a mold (a standard). If you fit into it, they are fine with you; you live above it, they will persecute you; if you live below it, they will punish you. If you are a believer and going through suffering, ask yourself if it is because of your faith in Christ. If not, then pray that God will deliver you from such evil: "And lead us not into temptation but deliver us from evil" (Matthew 6:13 ESV). If the answer is yes, pray that the Father delivers you from it lest you fall into temptation. In your prayer, submit to and ask the Father's will to be done. Jesus demonstrated this in Luke 22:40–46 (ESV):

> When he came to the place, he said to them, "Pray that you may not enter into temptation." And he withdrew from them about a stone's throw, and knelt down and prayed, **saying, "Father, if you are willing, remove this cup from me. Nevertheless, not my will, but yours, be done."** And there appeared to him an angel from heaven, strengthening him. And being in agony he prayed more earnestly; and his sweat became like great drops of blood falling down to the ground. And when he rose from prayer, he came to the disciples and found them sleeping for sorrow, **and he said to them, "Why are you sleeping? Rise and pray that you may not enter into temptation."**

Don't be ashamed of suffering because of your sonship:

> 1 Peter 4:14 (ESV)—If you are insulted for the name of Christ, you are blessed, because the Spirit of glory and of God rests upon you.

> Romans 8:17–18 (ESV)—And if children, then heirs—heirs of God and fellow heirs with Christ, provided we suffer with him in order that we may also be glorified with him. For I consider that the sufferings of this present time are not worth comparing with the glory that is to be revealed to us.

If God Is All-Powerful and Good, Why Is My Prayer Not Answered?

What if you have been praying for a long time and the problem, suffering, or painful circumstance is not going away? You may be asking, "Why should I suffer for that long if God is all-powerful?" I must admit that reality is on your side. I have seen people go to the mountains to pray, sometimes fast for days to have a child, and have a job to take care of their family after seeking a job again and again (although highly qualified). When I was trying to get to the university, my entrance exam result kept getting withheld for multiple years. I remember that I prayed, fasted, and worked again and again, but it seemed God was my enemy rather than a friend.

As a younger believer, I could not make sense of such woe and failure in life while actively serving God in the church choir. I was actively involved in the Royal Ambassador and Baptist Student Fellowship in the church. I was a leader among my colleagues in the church. I remember when one of my results came out for one of the examinations. I had worked so hard for it; it was all the same story. I watched my friend get into the university. I remember my church pastor, Reverend J. A. Adedeji, called me into his office to console me and teach me the ministry of presence. During that time, I learned that God allows things to happen so that He can work in us character and virtues that are requisite for His purpose in our lives. The virtues of patience, perseverance, endurance, and hope—the virtues of the Son's life—were being formed in me:

> Through him we have also obtained access by faith into this grace in which we stand, and we rejoice in hope of the glory of God. Not only that, but we rejoice in our sufferings, knowing that suffering produces endurance, and endurance produces character, and character produces hope, and hope does not put us to shame, because God's love has been poured into our hearts

through the Holy Spirit who has been given to us. (Romans 5:2–5 ESV)

Looking back today, I see how those years were instrumental to my ability to endure some of the painful experiences I have faced in my adult life.

You may be in a similar situation as well. Do not lose hope; God is forming the character of His Son in you, and when He is done, He will take the pain away. God's power is for God's purpose. When God has a purpose that He can fulfill and work together for good, keeping with the eternal working of His will to conform us to the image of Christ, He may not use His power to take away the pain. Doctors do this all the time, subjecting a patient to temporary pain to achieve a medically good purpose.

God seems to have abandoned Jesus on the cross; He appears to have left Job in sickness, boils, and calamities; God appears to be silent when James was beheaded. One would ask where He was when Stephen was being stoned to death. God seems to be watching and allowing those evil to occur. Why? It's because God sees how those occurrences work together for the good of the person going through it and His purpose of bringing many sons to glory. For example, Paul was there at Stephen's death. What if Paul needed to see Stephen's reaction while dying as part of God's working to get Paul ready for the Damascus encounter? Imagine how many sons of God have been brought to glory by Stephen's death if it contributed to Paul's conversion.

Look at the story of the birth of Jesus Christ. King Herod wanted to kill the Son of the all-powerful God, the God who created Herod. Jesus was God Himself. Rather than God using His power to stop Herod, He asked Mary and Joseph to run to Egypt. God running from a man. Killing Herod or protecting Jesus from Herod in Israel was not part of God's purpose and plan. The Messiah had to go down to Egypt for Him to be revealed as the Son of God who became the Christ. So you see how God did not use His power because using His power would have destroyed His purpose. The same thing happened to Moses when Pharaoh wanted to kill him. God instead allowed his mother to put him in the river to be discovered by Pharaoh's daughter because that will follow His purpose for Israel and His Son, Jesus Christ, and the plan to bring many sons to glory in the New Covenant.

Sometimes God will not use His infinite power to take away trouble from your life; instead, He might provide an alternative that may not appear supernatural, a solution that might be undesirable by you knowing the immeasurable power of God. Why would the God of Ephesians 3:20–21 not stop Herod and Pharaoh?

> Never doubt God's mighty power to work in you and accomplish all this. He will achieve infinitely more than your greatest request, your most unbelievable dream, and exceed your wildest imagination! He will outdo them all, for his miraculous power constantly energizes you. Now we offer up to God all the glorious praise that rises from every church in every generation through Jesus Christ— and all that will yet be manifest through time and eternity. Amen! (TPT)

You may be someone or know someone who has cancer, arthritis, COVID, who is barren, who has a genetic problem, who has all manner of sickness and disease, who is falsely imprisoned, who has been denied their pension or retirement rights, etc., that has caused prolonged pain and suffering. You might have seen ministers of God offer all manner of prayers and fasting over the situation, and it remains the same. Perhaps you are left wondering what God is doing. I will suggest a possible thing God is doing. If there is no perpetual unrepentant sin, God has allowed the situation and provided an alternative, seemingly natural way out because it is in line with His eternal good purpose for that person. God has found a way to supply grace to that person amid the pain while He is working to harvest many sons to glory as He reveals His

Son to many people and forms the image of His Son in the believer who is going through a bad situation. He might want you to see a doctor who will help you with cancer, cure the diseases, or talk to a lawyer that will guide you out of that court case so that those people might have the opportunity to interact with you to see and hear the gospel that leads to their salvation.

Those other means are all God's provision. This is not to misrepresent the fact that God wants to heal, save, deliver, and show up supernaturally—and He is still doing it to this day. Today might be your day if you can just ask God in faith. I recommend that you call on God now and cast your burden upon the Lord. And watch Him do the impossible in your life. In prayer, when you have sought the healing, breakthrough, and miracles by faith in the supernatural power of God, and nothing seems to be happening, ask yourself the question: what is the purpose that He is working on but I cannot currently see how it aligns with the path I have found myself on? God asked Jesus to get help from Egypt. He provided the basket and the river for Moses. God provided a wilderness for the man-child of Revelation 12 rather than kill the dragon immediately. Seek God's purpose so that you do not miss God's provision for you while He is working His eternal purpose with your situation. God did not rescue Joseph from His brothers but provided the Ishmaelites, Potiphar, the prison, and the king's cupbearer on His path for God's purpose for His son Israel—a chosen nation that will birth His Son, Jesus Christ. Psalm 105:15–22(TPT) shows through the life of Joseph what God might be doing amid the evil, pain, suffering, and calamity He allows:

> He said to them, "Don't you dare lay a hand on my anointed ones, and don't do a thing to hurt my prophets!" So God decreed a famine upon Canaan land, cutting off their food supply. But he had already sent a man ahead of his people to Egypt; it was Joseph, who was sold as a slave. His feet were bruised by strong shackles and his

soul was held by iron. God's promise to Joseph purged his character until it was time for his dreams to come true. Eventually, the king of Egypt sent for him, setting him free at last. Then Joseph was put in charge of everything under the king; he became the master of the palace over all of the royal possessions. Pharoah gave him authority over all the princes of the land, and Joseph became the teacher of wisdom to the king's advisers.

When Jesus was born, Mary and Joseph couldn't find a house or inn for the God of the universe to be delivered in. Why did God not use His power to create one supernaturally? In God's purpose, the Messiah had to be born in a manger to reveal Him as the bread of life and the Lamb of God that takes away the sin of the world. God did not take away the messenger of Satan sent to buffet Paul because God's purpose is to reveal His Son in Paul by keeping him humble. God does not want another "Devil" from a "Lucifer"—He instead wants the treasure of His Son in a jar of clay. When Lazarus was sick, Jesus waited for Him to die although He loved him: "So the sisters sent to him, saying, 'Lord, he whom you love is ill.' So, when he heard that Lazarus was ill, he stayed two days longer in the place where he was" (John 11:3, 6 ESV).

So Jesus loved him, yet He did not heal him of his sickness. Why? We already know that Jesus went about doing good, curing diseases and sickness, etc. Why the exception in this case?

In this case, Jesus knew that the Father had a purpose for allowing this particular sickness, and healing the illness right away would not achieve that purpose. Jesus expressed the purpose in John 11:4 (ESV): "But when Jesus heard it, he said, 'This illness does not lead to death. It is for the glory of God, so that the Son of God may be glorified through it.'"

The glory and revealing of the Son is the purpose and hope of creation. So if God sees and judges that a bad situation would allow for the Son to be glorified or for sons to be revealed, He will allow it. Jesus waited until Lazarus died and was in the grave for four days and then brought him back to life. Here is what He said:

John 11:42 (ESV)—"I knew that you always hear me, but I said this on account of the people standing around, **that they may believe that you sent me.**"

John 6:29 (ESV)—"Jesus answered them, '**This is the work of God, that you believe in him whom he has sent.**'"

So the work of God to reveal the Son and bring many sons to glory is also the reason for God allowing Lazarus to die. As soon as He accomplished God's purpose, he brought Lazarus back to life:

> When he had said these things, he cried out with a loud voice, "Lazarus, come out." The man who had died came out, his hands and feet bound with linen strips, and his face wrapped with a cloth. Jesus said to them, "Unbind him, and let him go"' (John 11:43–44 ESV).

God watched the three Hebrew boys be thrown into the fiery furnace although they stood for Him. Why? He saw that He would accomplish His purpose through the fiery furnace trial. What was that purpose? It was to reveal His Son:

> Daniel 3:25 (KJV)—"He answered and said, Lo, I see four men loose, walking in the midst of the fire, and they have no hurt; **and the form of the fourth is like the Son of God.**"

> Daniel 3:28 (KJV)—"Then Nebuchadnezzar spake, and said, Blessed be the God of Shadrach, Meshach, and Abednego, who hath sent his angel, and delivered his servants that trusted in him, and have changed the king's word, and yielded their bodies, that they might not serve nor worship any god, except their own God."

Imagine how much impact again it is to God for harvesting sons from the earth when the king of the superpower nation of that day sees the Son of God and believes. You can be in the midst of fire and be loosed if you can see the Son and God's purpose through your pain, suffering, sorrow, and death. One more person to look at is Job. The entire book of Job was the story of a righteous man who was afflicted with pain, sicknesses, evil, sorrow, suffering by the Devil, and God allowed it. Job lost everything, including his children, and God allowed the Devil to do it. God permitted the Devil to do it. After about forty plus chapters of suffering, persecution, and mental torture, God finally restored Job:

> And the LORD turned the captivity of Job, when he prayed for his friends: also the LORD gave Job twice as much as he had before. Then came there unto him all his brethren, and all his sisters, and all they that had been of his acquaintance before, and did eat bread with him in his house: and they bemoaned him, and comforted him over all the evil that the LORD had brought upon him [see an explanation for this phrase in Chapter 2]: every man also gave him a piece of money, and everyone an earring of gold. So the LORD blessed the latter end of Job more than his beginning: for he had fourteen thousand sheep, and six thousand camels, and a thousand yoke of oxen, and a thousand she asses. He had also seven sons and three daughters. And he called the name of the first, Jemima; and the name of the second, Kezia; and the name of the third, Keren-happuch. And in all the land were no women found so fair as the daughters of Job: and their father gave them inheritance among their brethren. After this lived Job an hundred and forty years, and saw his sons, and his sons' sons, even four generations. So Job died, being old and full of days. (Job 42:10–17 KJV)

Here is an excellent example of a good man, a righteous man, and an innocent man that evil happened to; it lingered for a while, and God finally responded to his cry. I studied the book of Job very carefully for what it was that made

God wait for forty-plus chapters before restoring Job's fortune. I found my answer in Job 42. It was the exact purpose of revealing and forming His Son. God wanted to reveal His Son in Job to shame the Devil that He will accomplish His purpose ultimately.

The Devil came at the time that the sons of God were gathered in God's presence: "Now there was a day when the **sons of God** came to present themselves before the LORD, and Satan came also among them" (Job 1:6 KJV).

God started bragging on Job that he was one son of man that God could work in to become a son of God. Job loved righteousness and hated wickedness like Jesus: "You have loved righteousness and hated wickedness; therefore God, your God, has set you above your companions by anointing you with the oil of joy" (Hebrews 1:9 NIV).

In Job 1:8 (KJV), we read, "And the LORD said unto Satan, Hast thou considered my servant Job, that there is none like him in the earth, a perfect and an upright man, one that feareth God, and escheweth evil?'"

Satan wanted Job to fail to prove to God that there was no hope for Him to accomplish His purpose for sonship. Satan wanted Job to betray and deny God like he wanted Jesus to do in the wilderness:

> Then Satan answered the LORD, and said, "Doth Job fear God for nought? Hast not thou made an hedge about him, and about his house, and about all that he hath on every side? thou hast blessed the work of his hands, and his substance is increased in the land. But put forth thine hand now, and touch all that he hath, and he will curse thee to thy face." And the LORD said unto Satan, "Behold, all that he hath is in thy power; only upon himself put not forth thine hand." So, Satan went forth from the presence of the LORD. (Job 1:9–12 KJV)

That discourse began the suffering of Job. Do you see a type of Christ in Job? He suffered for no sin of His own. He was a man who refused to partner with the Devil and evil, yet sons of men persecuted him. However, there was a quiet pride, a quiet self-exaltation and self-righteousness in Job that took God over forty chapters to reveal and take away so that He could boldly say about Job to the Devil—this is a type of my Son, and I am pleased with him. So God could brag about Job on the Devil to accomplish His purpose in Christ.

Now, when did God restore the fortune of Job? Job proved himself a viable candidate to be a son of God on the earth. He was rid of self-adoration—which could make him become a Devil like Lucifer. He was emptied of self:

> Then Job answered the LORD, and said, I know that thou canst do everything, and that no thought can be withholden from thee. Who is he that hideth counsel without knowledge? therefore have I uttered that I understood not; things too wonderful for me, which I knew not. Hear, I beseech thee, and I will speak: I will demand of thee, and declare thou unto me. I have heard of thee by the hearing of the ear: but now mine eye seeth thee. Wherefore I abhor my**self** and repent in dust and ashes (Job 42:1–6 KJV, emphasis mine).

Job saw the Lord and became like Him: "Beloved, now are we the sons of God, and it doth not yet appear what we shall be: but we know that, when he shall appear, we shall be like him; for we shall see him as he is" (1 John 3:2 KJV).

Job acquired the mind of Christ when he saw the Lord. Philippians 2:5–11(ESV)describe the mind of Christ:

> **Have this mind among yourselves, which is yours in Christ Jesus,** who, though he was in the form of God, did not count equality with God a thing to be grasped, **but emptied himself,** by taking the form of a servant, being born in the likeness of men. And being found in human form, he humbled himself by becoming obedient to the point of death, even death on a cross. Therefore God has highly exalted him and bestowed on him the

name that is above every name, so that at the name of Jesus every knee should bow, in heaven and on earth and under the earth, and every tongue confess that Jesus Christ is Lord, to the glory of God the Father.

Just like God exalted Jesus Christ, He also restored the fortune of Job. All through the book of Job, Job appeared that he was grasping his righteousness as if to claim equality with God. But in the last chapter, he learned the humble mind of Christ. So until God accomplished His purpose of sonship in Job, the calamity remained, but somehow, He gave Job grace amid the fire until the Son of God was revealed to him. To confirm that God was working sonship in Job for which He allowed the suffering to linger, Job 42:10 shows us another thing about sonship that God had accomplished: "And the LORD restored the fortunes of Job **when he had prayed for his friends**. And the LORD gave Job twice as much as he had before."

When you read Job 42:10, you will think Job was praying for friendly friends. Not really—he was praying for those who had mocked, questioned his righteousness, and despitefully used him earlier in the book of Job. When did God restore his fortune? *When he prayed for his friends* (those who had persecuted him). Here Job demonstrated his sonship

> "You have heard that it was said, 'You shall love your neighbor and hate your enemy.' But I say to you, **Love your enemies and pray for those who persecute you, so that you may be sons of your Father who is in heaven**. For he makes his sun rise on the evil and on the good and sends rain on the just and on the unjust. (Matthew 5:43–45 ESV)

We see again from the life of Job that God's power is for God's purpose. We see that pain and suffering may be allowed by God if it will lead to revealing, manifesting, forming, and producing the Son of God on the earth. In this chapter, I have shown what God revealed to me for why He allows pain, suffering, and calamity in the lives of good people and why God seems silent during such a problem. Evil, pain, and suffering exist in this world because we live in a broken world under the power of evil, and humans have had an evil nature since the fall of Adam. The Devil is constantly trying to afflict men—like the story of Job—to ensure we cannot become sons of God. On the side of God, He is good and wants to do good on the earth. The summary of it all is this: God is never unaware or indifferent during such a situation.

1. He is counting on His ministers and sons to deal with evil.
2. He sees how the situation can lead to the harvesting of sons from the earth—which is His eternal good purpose for which creation exists.
3. God is working behind the scenes to accomplish His eternal purpose.
4. He always provides alternative coping routes till the time His purpose is accomplished.
5. He supplies grace through it all.
6. If and when His purpose of sonship is accomplished in each situation, He will use His supernatural power to change the situation.

Ultimately, God's power is for God's purpose, and He is not under obligation to use His power to change a situation if it thwarts His purpose. He is, however, constantly working all things to fulfill His purpose by His power:

> Romans 8:28 (ESV) — " And we know that for those who love God all things **work together for good, for those who are called according to his purpose**."

> Ephesians 1:11(ESV) — "In him we have obtained an inheritance, having been predestined according to the **purpose of him who works all things according to the counsel of his will…**

Chapter Twelve

We Have This Hope as an Anchor

Surviving the Storm of Life

Hebrews 6:19–20 (TPT) reads,

> We have this certain hope like a strong, unbreakable anchor holding our souls to God himself. **Our anchor of hope is fastened to the mercy seat** which sits in the heavenly realm beyond the sacred threshold, and where Jesus, our forerunner, has gone in before us. He is now and forever our royal Priest like Melchizedek.

This chapter is for you! It is for you who first hoped and believed in God for the salvation of your soul. It is for you who once unashamedly hoped in God, but life situations have made you wonder if you could hold on any longer. Hang on, stay with me through this chapter, and I trust God that hope will rekindle in your heart as you lay hold of the promises of God.

Hope is particularly important to our existence. When there is no hope, there is anxiety and depression. Lack of hope can bring despair and suicide. Hopelessness is the fertilizer of many of the misbehavior and vices that we see around us today. On the other hand, when hope is alive, there is faith, joy, peace, and harmony. The importance of hope could be illustrated with childbirth. A mother endures all the pain of childbirth, even when the baby's arrival seems to tear her apart. What keeps her going is the hope of a newborn baby. Nothing in creation can work as God designed it without hope. All the bondages in creation are being endured because creation itself is hoping for the birth of the sons of God. The survival of creation is hinging on the virtue of hope; otherwise, creation would have been torn apart and in permanent bondage and complete, utter meaninglessness. Romans 8:19–21 shows us how important hope is!

> For the earnest expectation of the creature waiteth for the manifestation of the sons of God. For the creature was made subject to vanity, not willingly, but by reason of him who hath subjected the same in hope, Because the creature itself also shall be delivered from the bondage of corruption into the glorious liberty of the children of God. (Romans 8:19-21 KJV)

Even Jesus was able to endure the cross because He had hope in what will happen after the resurrection, the hope of bringing forth sons of God from the earth:

> Looking unto Jesus the author and finisher of our faith; **who for the joy that was set before him** endured the cross, despising the shame, and is set down at the right hand of the throne of God. (Hebrews 12:2 KJV)

It is extremely difficult to keep the faith and keep fighting when there is no hope. There cannot be faith when there is no hope, and hope emanates from faithful promises. Our God is a God of faithful promises that bring hope. He is the God who made a promise to Abraham and fulfilled His promise to him. Hebrews 6:13–20 (TPT) shows us the nature of God's promise that brings living hope for which our faith is the substance:

Now when God **made a promise to Abraham,** since there was no one greater than himself, **he swore an oath on his own integrity to keep the promise as sure as God exists! So he said, "Have no doubt, I promise to bless you over and over,** and give you a son and multiply you without measure!" So Abraham waited patiently in faith and succeeded in seeing the promise fulfilled. It is very common for people to swear an oath by something greater than themselves, **for the oath will confirm their statements and end all dispute. So in the same way, God wanted to end all doubt and confirm it even more forcefully to those who would inherit his promises. His purpose was unchangeable, so God added his vow to the promise.** So **it is impossible for God to lie for we know that his promise and his vow will never change!** And now we have run into his heart to hide ourselves in his faithfulness. **This is where we find his strength and comfort, for he empowers us to seize what has already been established ahead of time—an unshakable hope! We have this certain hope like a strong, unbreakable anchor holding our souls to God himself. Our anchor of hope is fastened to the mercy seat which sits in the heavenly realm beyond the sacred threshold,** and where Jesus, our forerunner, has gone in before us. He is now and forever our royal Priest like Melchizedek.

There is hope for those who are heirs of the same promise that God made to Abraham and fulfilled in Christ Jesus—period! God's faithful promises are the source of our hope. As an example of the nature of God's promises that keep hope alive, Hebrews 6:13–20 (TPT) shows us how this works.

1. Our God is a God of faithful promises (verse 13,18).
2. God backed His promise up with an oath (verses 13, 17, 18).

3. God added a vow to the promises to end all dispute that His promise will come to pass (verse 16, 17).
4. God swore the oath on His integrity since no one is greater than Him (verse 13).
5. God wants to bless us— the seeds of Abraham— by faith (verse 14).

These scriptures show that His promises will come to pass since God exists and has sworn by Himself. And these promises give us hope, and the hope of God's promises is like an unbreakable anchor holding our souls to God Himself. Our hope is fastened to the mercy seat, which sits in the heavenly realm beyond the sacred threshold, and where Jesus, our forerunner, has gone in before us. In other words, like a ship in the storm held firm by an anchor, we can stand firm in the storms of life by having faith as the substance of the hope we have in the promise of God. We have this hope as an anchor. God indeed fulfilled His promise to Abraham. God wants to do good to and bless those who are the seed of Abraham— and those of us who have put our faith in Jesus Christ are the seeds of Abraham. Therefore, we have been blessed with faithful Abraham's blessing. As God swore to Abraham in Genesis 17, He has sworn on a greater covenant to us that He will be more than a God to us. He will be our Father as well:

> Hosea 1:10 (ESV)—"Yet the number of the children of Israel shall be like the sand of the sea, which cannot be measured or numbered. And in the place where it was said to them, 'You are not my people,' it shall be said to them, 'Children of the living God.'"

> 2 Corinthians 6:18 (ESV)—"And I will be a father to you, and you shall be sons and daughters to me, says the Lord Almighty."

As children of God, the God who is good and has made faithful promises that He has backed up with an oath, we can hope in Him. If an earthly father who has an evil nature of iniquity can give good gifts to their children, much more can we put our hope in God, our heavenly Father who is all good and with no evil in Him at all? He has promised He will never fail us.

Regardless of what you might be going through at this moment in your life, because of whom we know God our Father to be, we can say like Job, "If a man dies, shall he live again? all the days of my appointed time will I wait, till my change come" (Job 14:14 KJV)—leaning on His faithfulness and goodness.

Change is coming—God has the power to change things. He has made promises. He is good and cannot lie. Our God is a God of hope (Romans 15:13). According to Job, even trees that are cut have hope of sprouting again: "For **there is hope for a tree** if it be cut down, that it will sprout again, and that its shoots will not cease" (Job 14:7 ESV).

So we can rejoice in Him as we persevere and be patient in the hope for Him to fulfill His promise. Romans 5:2–5 shows that hope in God does not disappoint or make us ashamed:

> By whom also we have access by faith into this grace wherein we stand and **rejoice in hope** of the glory of God. And not only so, but we glory in tribulations also: knowing that tribulation worketh patience. And patience, experience; and experience, hope: And **hope maketh not ashamed**; because the love of God is shed abroad in our hearts by the Holy Ghost which is given unto us. (KJV)

We can wait and hope in God, our Redeemer. We know He lives, and we will see His goodness in the land of the living. We shall see for ourselves when he will fulfill His promises to us:

For I know that my Redeemer lives, and at the last he will stand upon the earth. And after my skin has been thus destroyed, yet in my flesh I shall see God, whom I shall see for myself, and my eyes shall behold, and not another. My heart faints within me! (Job 19:25–27 ESV)

No matter how bad your situation might be, we serve a God who gives life to the dead. By faith, as the substance of the hope we have in His promise, which we did nothing to earn, we will receive His salvation, blessings, breakthrough, deliverance, healing, and life. Romans 4:16–21 (ESV) shows us that the promise of God to Abraham was this source of his hope.—and he is the Father of us all:

Romans 4:16 (ESV)—"That is why **it depends on faith, in order that the promise may rest on grace** and be guaranteed to all his offspring—not only to the adherent of the law but also to the one who shares the faith of Abraham, who is the father of us all."

Abraham was so strong in the promise of God that his hope transcended all hope. He had the hope that defied hopeless reality:

Romans 4:18 (ESV)—"In **hope he believed against hope, that he should become the father of many nations,** as he had been told, 'So shall your offspring be.'"

The promise of God was sufficient for Abraham. His anchor held firm even when the storms showed hopelessness. He had unwavering hope because he did not doubt that God was faithful enough to do what He say and only say what He would do—because He cannot lie.

Romans 4:19–21 (ESV)—"He **did not weaken in faith** when he considered his own body, which was as good as dead (since he was about a hundred years old), or when he considered the barrenness of Sarah's womb. No **unbelief made him waver concerning the promise of God**, but he grew strong in his faith as he gave glory to God fully **convinced that God was able to do what he had promised**."

This is the same Abraham who did not see the promise of God come to pass for twenty-five plus years. He was already one hundred years old and his wife ninety years old. Yet he kept believing God's promise and therefore kept hope alive. Even when Sarah medically couldn't conceive nor had the strength to give birth, Abraham rested on the hope of God's promise. Abraham knew that when God speaks, it is done. He knew that our God is the God of the living and the dead, and He gives life to the dead and calls into existence the things that do not exist. (Romans 4:17b). The God of Abraham, the Father of our Lord Jesus Christ, is the God we also serve, and He never changes.

God demonstrated His faithfulness to give life to the dead even in His incarnation in Christ Jesus. He is the resurrection and the life. He specializes in giving life to anything dead. In other words, He is an expert when it comes to bringing hope out of hopeless situations. When the best of men can no longer fix it, please take it to Jesus. When it defies all medical, logical, and scientific solutions, take it to Dr. Jesus—God incarnate. The man of Calvary is the resurrection and the life.

The story of Lazarus is an excellent example of God giving life to a dead situation and soul. In the gospel according to John 11:1–44, we read the story of a man by the name of Lazarus. Lazarus was sick and dying. I guess no medical solution was available to help him. His sisters reached out to Dr. Jesus. Counterintuitively, Jesus waited two more days so that Lazarus died. By the time Jesus got to Bethany, Lazarus had been dead for four days—"By this time, he stinketh: for he hath been dead four days" (John 11:39). In other words, his case was now hopeless. Has anyone ever heard a man that has died for four days come back to life? Not until this time. Lazarus's predicament was an impossible case and hopeless. Jesus made it clear to Mary and Martha that He was the resurrection and the life:

> Jesus said unto her, "**I am the resurrection, and the life: he that believeth in me, though he were dead, yet shall he live:** And whosoever liveth and believeth in me shall never die. Believest thou this?" She saith unto him, "Yea, Lord: I believe that thou art the Christ, the Son of God, which should come into the world." (John 11:25–27 ESV)

Like Martha, some of us understand the hope of resurrection to eternal life in the last day—which is accurate, and we should look forward to it: "Martha saith unto him, 'I know that he shall rise again in the resurrection at the last day'" (John 11:24KJV).

We will discuss that in the final chapter of this book. However, Jesus was not talking about that future blessed hope in Lazarus's story. Jesus was dealing with the hope of resurrection in the here and now when he said, "Thy brother shall rise again" (John 11:23 KJV).

We must understand that our God is the God of hope not just in the future resurrection state but in the here and now. Are you willing to believe with me in the God who quickens the dead in the here and now, although He will still do it in the future?

John 5:25 (KJV)—"Verily, verily, I say unto you, **The hour is coming, and now is, when the dead shall hear the voice of the Son of God: and they that hear shall live.**"

What a hope that resurrection life is in the here and now. You know the rest of Lazarus's story. Jesus literally fulfilled this statement in John 5:25 when he called Lazarus forth.

John 11:43 (KJV)—"And when he thus had spoken, he cried with a loud voice, **Lazarus, come forth.**"

Jesus revealed the glory of God—Christ in you, the hope of glory (Colossians 1:27–29). He showed His sonship when He called Lazarus to life (see John 5:25 and John 11:43). I believe Jesus Christ, who is the same, yesterday, today, and forevermore (Hebrews 13:8), wants to reveal His sonship in your hopeless situation and circumstance. He has promised that even the dead would hear His voice and live, and He cannot lie. We can hope in His promise. I believe our God is filling your heart and entire being with what He has in abundance—it is called hope.

Romans 15:13 (KJV)—"**Now the God of hope fill you** with all joy and peace in believing, that ye may abound in hope, through the power of the Holy Ghost."

Like Mary and Martha, do you believe in the hope of resurrection in the here and now? That God wants to bring life to your "dead Lazarus type situations"—even if it stinketh by now. **Believest Thou This?** (John 11:26 KJV). If you do, bring the situation to Him now. Call on Him, the God of all hope, the God who gives life to the dead—call on Him now. Taste and see that the Lord is good. I join my faith with yours that your time has come! It is your time to know the resurrection power of Jesus. It is time for God to turn your hopeless case around. There shall be a testimony of the revelation of God's Son in your circumstance in Jesus's name.

When the Lord has turned your captivity around, "Loose him and let him go." Loose him and let him go by making the work of God plain for all to see that He is good. Share the testimony of His goodness on the rooftop. Let all see what the Lord has done. Let them know that the Son of God is alive, and He is still doing wonders and turning the hopeless situation around. Let the "priests" see it and confirm that Jesus has healed your "leprosy." By that, I mean get medical confirmation and any necessary evidence to show that God has healed you, turned your situation around, that God has fought on your behalf and has kept His promises and has done the impossible in your life. Tell the whole world, "Come and see what our good Lord has done; there is nothing he cannot do."

> Jeremiah 32:27 (KJV)—"Behold, I am the LORD, the God of all flesh: **is there anything too hard for me?**"

> Matthew 19:26 (KJV)—"But Jesus beheld them, and said unto them, 'With men this is impossible, but **with God all things are possible**.'"

> Luke 1:37 (KJV)—"For **with God nothing shall be impossible**."

Even if your case is like that of Jabez, you can call on God, and He will grant what you ask per His will to bless you as He promised faithful Abraham. God will turn your situation around as you ask Him and seek His kingdom first:

> Jabez was more honorable than his brothers; and his mother called his name Jabez, saying, "Because I bore him in pain." Jabez called upon the God of Israel, saying, "Oh that you would bless me and enlarge my border, and that your hand might be with me, and that you would keep me from harm so that it might not bring me pain!" **And God granted what he asked.** (1 Chronicles 4:9–10 ESV)

> Hebrews 11:6 (KJV)—"But without faith, it is impossible to please him: **for he that cometh to God must believe that he is, and that he is a rewarder of them that diligently seek him.**"

> Hebrews 11:1 (KJV)—"**Now faith is the substance of things hoped for,** the evidence of things not seen."

> John 11:40 (KJV)—"Jesus said to her, **'Did I not tell you that if you believed you would see the glory of God?'**"

As I was working on the edit of this chapter for the first draft of this book, something miraculous happened. I led a small group in my church; a lady in the group called me on December 19, 2021, to say that her husband had tested positive for COVID-19. At that time, he was in the ICU, already on a ventilator. As soon as she told us, my wife and I began to pray immediately. We began to speak the resurrection life of Jesus into all of the parts of his body. We began to send His promise in Romans 8:11 to our friend's body: "If the Spirit of him who raised Jesus from the dead dwells in you, he who raised Christ Jesus from the dead will also give life to your mortal bodies through His Spirit who dwells in you."

As soon as we stopped praying, we contacted our group members and the director of connect group to let the family care team know. A few hours later, we heard from his wife that his situation started to change. The next day, December 20, 2021, he was taken off the ventilator. As I write today, December 28, 2021, my friend is going home from the hospital. Our Jesus is the resurrection and the life.

I will end this section by quoting from Bro. Gbile Akanni: *"The resurrection and the life is here."* He is here for *you* to turn your hopeless situation around! Believest thou this? There is a promise of hope in Jeremiah 29:11: "'For I know the plans I have for you,' declares the LORD, 'plans to prosper you and not to harm you, **plans to give you hope** and a future.'"

Our God is a God of faithful promises and a God of hope. There are several promises in the Bible that your hope can rest on. His promises are Yes and Amen.

> 2 Corinthians 1:19—20 "For the Son of God, Jesus Christ, whom we proclaimed among you, Silvanus and Timothy and I, was not Yes and No, but in him it is always Yes. **For all the promises of God find their Yes in him. That is why it is through him that we utter our Amen to God for his glory.**"

God wants to give you hope, and this hope comes from His faithful promises. Your faith in those promises keeps hope alive.

What hopeless situation do you need God to change? His promises are His commitment to you. Put your hope in His promises and watch Him prove himself faithful and good. You can say amen to all His promises in the Bible. You can search the Bible, use a concordance, search online, or buy resources that contain God's promises. They will give you hope, which will become an anchor to your soul while you wait for God to show up in supernatural power to change your situation. Below are some other examples of God's promises to you:

> Matthew 6:31–33—"**So do not worry**, saying, 'What shall we eat?' or 'What shall we drink?' or 'What shall we wear?' For the pagans run after all these things, and your heavenly Father knows that you need them. **But seek first his kingdom and his righteousness, and all these things will be given to you as well."**

> Matthew 11:28–30—"**Come to me, all you who are weary and burdened, and I will give you rest.** Take my yoke upon you and learn from me, for I am gentle and humble in heart, and you will find rest for your souls. For my yoke is easy and my burden is light."

> 2 Corinthians 9:8—"And **God is able to bless you abundantly, so that in all things at all times, having all that you need, you will abound in every good work."**

> Romans 8:32—"He who did not spare his own Son, but gave him up for us all—how will he not also, along with him, graciously give us all things?"

James 1:5—"If any of you lacks wisdom, you should ask God, who gives generously to all without finding fault, and it will be given to you."
Mark 11:24—"Therefore I tell you, whatever you ask for in prayer, believe that you have received it, and it will be yours."

Psalm 37:4—"Take delight in the Lord, and he will give you the desires of your heart."

John 14:13—"And I will do whatever you ask in my name, so that the Father may be glorified in the Son. You may ask me for anything in my name, and I will do it."

Luke 11:9–13—"So I say to you: Ask and it will be given to you; seek and you will find; knock and the door will be opened to you. For everyone who asks receives; the one who seeks finds; and to the one who knocks, the door will be opened. Which of you fathers, if your son asks for a fish, will give him a snake instead? Or if he asks for an egg, will give him a scorpion? If you then, though you are evil, know how to give good gifts to your children, how much more will your Father in heaven give the Holy Spirit to those who ask him!"

Psalm 23:1–6—"The LORD is my shepherd; I shall not want. He maketh me to lie down in green pastures: he leadeth me beside the still waters. He restoreth my soul: he leadeth me in the paths of righteousness for his name's sake. Yea, though I walk through the valley of the shadow of death, I will fear no evil: for thou art with me; thy rod and thy staff they comfort me. Thou preparest a table before me in the presence of mine enemies: thou anointest my head with oil; my cup runneth over. Surely goodness and mercy shall follow me all the days of my life: and I will dwell in the house of the LORD forever."

Psalm 103:1–5—"Bless the LORD, O my soul, and all that is within me, bless his holy name! Bless the LORD, O my soul, and forget not all his benefits, who forgives all your iniquity, who heals all your diseases, who redeems your life from the pit, who crowns you with steadfast love and mercy, **who satisfies you with good** so that your youth is renewed like the eagle's."

We can have hope in our good God. He plans to give us hope and a future. He desires to satisfy us with good and renew our strength. While you are waiting for God to show up in power for your situation, keep praise and rejoice in hope:

Though the fig tree should not blossom, nor fruit be on the vines, the produce of the olive fail and the fields yield no food, the flock be cut off from the fold and there be no herd in the stalls, yet I will rejoice in the LORD; I will take joy in the God of my salvation. GOD, the Lord, is my strength; he makes my feet like the deer's; he makes me tread on my high places. To the choirmaster: with stringed instruments. (Habakkuk 3:17–19)

The Devil plans to steal your joy by stealing your hope. Satan is not so much interested in afflicting your things; he is interested in your heart, to make it hopeless so that you are rid of the joy of the Lord and become weak. Satan knows that the joy of the Lord is your strength. Do you know this?

Then he said unto them, Go your way, eat the fat, and drink the sweet, and send portions unto them for whom nothing is prepared: for this day is holy unto our Lord: neither be ye sorry; **for the joy of the LORD is your strength**. (Nehemiah 8:10)

If you are going through suffering as a child of God, keep hope. Let Hebrews 10, 11, and 12 be an encouragement to you:

Cast not away therefore your confidence, which hath great recompence of reward. For ye have need of patience, that, after ye have done the will of God, ye might receive the promise. For yet a little while, and he that shall come will come, and will not tarry. Now the just shall live by faith: but if any man draw back, my soul shall have no pleasure in him. But we are not of them who draw back unto perdition; but of them that believe to the saving of the soul. (Hebrews 10:35–39)

Consider the life of men gone before who endured till the end in Hebrews 11 and let their endurance and perseverance and hope be a motivation for you to keep keeping on and keep hope alive:

Looking unto Jesus the author and finisher of our faith; who for the joy that was set before him endured the cross, despising the shame, and is set down at the right hand of the throne of God. (Hebrews 12:2 KJV)

Let us pray. It's time to pray and bring all impossible and hopeless situations to Jesus. You don't have to have your diction and grammar correct and perfectly quote all scripture. You just have to believe as the substance of your hope in His promise. He will reward your diligence, persistence, and faith in Him and His goodness.

Chapter Thirteen

He Is Making All Things New

Ultimate Bliss and Eternal Hope

It has been a long ride leading up to this chapter. We spent a significant part of this book understanding that God alone is good, and all good and perfect gifts come from Him. In chapter 2, I argued that it makes sense that God can be good while evil exists today, and that God has a plan to deal with evil in time and for all eternity. Chapters 3 and 4 were dedicated to arguing for the existence of God and the reliability of the Bible. Hopefully, if you were an atheist or someone who does not believe in the Bible, you have crossed to the other side of firm belief in the existence of God and the accuracy, historical credibility, and inerrancy of the Bible.

There are scriptural verses in the Bible that speak to God's goodness. Below are examples of such verses of scriptures all in ESV translation:

> 1 Chronicles 16:34—"**Oh give thanks to the LORD, for he is good**; for his steadfast love endures forever!"

> Psalm 31:19—"Oh, **how abundant is your goodness**, which you have stored up for those who fear you and worked for those who take refuge in you, in the sight of the children of mankind!"

Psalm 34:8—"Oh, **taste and see that the LORD is good!** Blessed is the man who takes refuge in him!"

Psalm 86:5—"**For you, O Lord, are good** and forgiving, abounding in steadfast love to all who call upon you."

Psalm 100:5—"**For the LORD is good;** his steadfast love endures forever, and his faithfulness to all generations."

Psalm 107:1—"**Oh give thanks to the LORD, for he is good,** for his steadfast love endures forever!"

Psalm 145:9—"**The LORD is good to all**, and his mercy is over all that he has made."

Nahum 1:7—"**The LORD is good, a stronghold in the day of trouble**; he knows those who take refuge in him."

Romans 8:28—"And we know that for those who love **God all things work together for good,** for those who are called according to his purpose."

James 1:17—"**Every good gift and every perfect gift is from above, coming down from the Father of lights,** with whom there is no variation or shadow due to change."

The Bible has more verses that speak of the goodness of God. Search the scriptures to find them and apply your heart to them. It is clear from the testimony of more than three witnesses of the scriptures above that God is good! And He is good to all. Since He is good, we can run to Him in days of evil, trouble, calamity, and woes. We can call upon Him and receive a good gift from God who dwells above. I call you today to try the Lord by believing Him to do you good in whatever situation. As you would a new restaurant to see if their food is good, taste and see that the Lord is good.

God is so good—good must have come from Him. Otherwise, where does all the goodness we see and enjoy in creation come from? When you look throughout the whole course of creation, existence, history of life, humanity, the story of the universe, from where does all the good we know come? Where does all the good you have seen come from—all the love, kindness, joy, fun, and excitement?

When you go to the water park or when you go bungee jumping. Just think about it at the beach and ocean. You sit beside the sea, and you just see the calmness of the ocean and the cool breeze that blows all over you with sweet and good sensation, serenity, and peace. Think about all the good food and meals that you eat. What about all the pleasant sounds and music from jazz, blues, acapella, afrobeat, juju, reggae, samba, to classical music? I am not mainly talking yet about the arranged song with lyrics in those genres, which we might disagree on the content of the lyrics. I am simply talking about the soothing feeling that music sound brings to us. I mean the therapeutic effect of the music. Think of all the musical instruments that give lovely sound to your ears—instruments like saxophones, trumpets, drum sets, keyboard pianos, guitars, etc.

Think about all of creation and the things that God has made and the things that exist in nature and all the beauty. What about the magnificence of water? We drink from it and wash our bodies and clothes with it to stay clean and healthy. We swim in it for relaxation and fun. People even have hydrotherapy that can bring some form of healing to them with water. The sunlight, beautiful skies, and natural phenomenon for us to behold tell of His goodness. All the evil in nature is because of the bondage the Devil puts it in, and all the good things we see are the remnant of the state of the universe that God first created when He said: "It is good."

These examples of good things in life that I mentioned exist in creation that is still under bondage to evil. Can you then imagine what God has in stock for us when all evil is eradicated? Imagine what this good God wanted to offer humanity—it was good, is good, and will be good alone. So if you doubt the goodness of God, let all of these beautiful things that God has created tell you about His goodness. The Bible says in Psalm 19:1–5,

> For the Pure and Shining One. A poem of praise by King David, his loving servant. God's splendor is a tale that is told; his testament is written in the stars. Space itself speaks his story every day through the marvels of the heavens. His truth is on tour in the starry vault of the sky, showing his skill in creation's craftsmanship. Each day gushes out its message to the next, night with night whispering its knowledge to all. Without a sound, without a word, without a voice being heard, yet all the World can see its story. Everywhere its gospel is clearly read so all may know. What a heavenly home God has set for the sun, shining in the superdome of the sky! See how he leaves his celestial chamber each morning, radiant as a bridegroom ready for his wedding, like a day-breaking champion eager to run his course.

The whole creation expresses His goodness to us. We have natural herbs within God's creation that heal and relieve pain and suffering. All scientific and medical breakthroughs that have made human life worth living and enjoyable have all come fundamentally from God's creation—how can He not be good? It will be unfair to say that God is evil or authored evil in light of all the good things that we could enjoy from creation as God daily loads us with the benefit of His goodness in creation. We can foolishly choose to attribute evil to God or we can face the fact of existence and tell the Devil to his face that he is a disgrace to God's creation. We need to remind the Devil that he was made good and excellent like all creation, but he messed up and deserves God's eternal judgment in the fire.

Can we express to God that we can see now? We can perceive correctly now. Our eyes are open to see. We now know to see the problem of evil for what it is—that God is good and He only does good and that the Devil is the author of all evil acts. Like they say in my culture, the masquerade is unveiled; we can see what is beneath the mask. God is good, God is good, and I dare to say it louder and louder to all those who care to listen—God is good, and He only does good.

As I was preparing this section, my wife reminded me of the need to include Jeremiah 29:11 in this section. This verse shows us that God has thoughts about creation and humanity—they are good thoughts. He has never thought evil about all of His creation. God did not learn to start thinking good—He is eternally omniscient, and He never changes. He has always been thinking the same. What does that tell us? Before He created anything, He only had thoughts of good; that's why His desire is the driving force for good, just like thought and the desire for selfishness outside of the focus on God is what is the driving force for evil. When God looks at you before you were born, He sees a creature worthy of enjoying His goodness:

> There is no such thing as darkness with you. The night, to you, is as bright as the day; there's no difference between the two. You formed my innermost being, shaping my delicate inside and my intricate outside, and wove them all together in my mother's womb. I thank you, God, for making me so mysteriously complex! Everything you do is marvelously breathtaking. It simply amazes me to think about it! How thoroughly you know me, Lord! You even formed every bone in my body when you created me in the secret place, carefully, skillfully shaping me from nothing to something. You saw who you created me to be before I became me! Before I'd ever seen the light of day, the number of days you planned for me were already recorded in your book. **Every single moment you are thinking of me! How precious and wonderful to consider that you cherish me**

constantly in your every thought! O God, your desires toward me are more than the grains of sand on every shore! When I awake each morning, you're still with me. (Psalm 139:12–18)

God said He had your thoughts in mind before you had one day and all the days of your life, and they are written in His book. We may not understand all the specific intricacies behind why God allows certain anomalies in childbirth. However, as explained earlier in this book, He has a purpose behind it, and it is a good one. We can trust that His thought about everyone and every situation is for good. If we follow the script of God's design, which is the path of following Jesus that brings rest, we will only experience His goodness—His goodness is always running after us. And even when we go through the fire as we follow Him, the effect of the suffering will lose its power as it did with the three Hebrew men in the furnace of fire.

God plans to lead us beside still water, even if His rod and staff comfort us. He restores our souls when we walk through or He leads us through the wilderness of life. If your soul is going through pain, if your soul is in agony, follow and allow God to lead you. He will lead you to freshwater that will comfort your soul (2 Corinthians 1:3–4). He will show you His goodness where there are green pastures.

Jesus is the good shepherd (John 10:1–16). He will always lay His life down for you. As the good shepherd, He has His rod and the staff to guide and keep you on the path of His goodness. He has planned good works for you before the foundation of the world:

Ephesians 2:10—"For we are his workmanship, created in Christ Jesus **unto good works, which God hath before ordained that we should walk in them.**

Ephesians 2:10 (AMPC)—"For we are God's [own] handiwork [His workmanship, recreated in Christ Jesus

249

[born anew], that we may do those good works which God predestined [planned beforehand] for us **[taking paths which He prepared ahead of time], that we should walk in them"** [living the good life which He prearranged and made ready for us to live].

God will lead you on the path toward His goodness in this broken world. God knows the path of His goodness in this degenerated world. God knows the path of His goodness in this world of disorder. God knows the path of His goodness, and He sometimes uses His rod and staff to keep us in the green pasture of His goodness. He keeps us out of the path of "lions", "wolves', and "hyenas' of this world. He keeps us away from the power and domain of the demons and the Devil. As the good shepherd, in His goodness, He delivers us from evil.

Regardless of what you are going through now, do not walk away from God into the hand of the Devil. The suffering of this present time pales in comparison to the goodness that God has in store for you in the now and the hereafter.

1 Corinthians 2:9 (KJV)—"But as it is written, Eye hath not seen, nor ear heard, neither have entered into the heart of man, the things which God hath prepared for them that love him."

Trust in God's plan and desire for you. Never forget that God said He has a thought toward you for good and a glorious hope and future. Be encouraged by 1 Peter 5:7–10 (TPT):

> Give all your worries and cares to God, for he cares about you. Stay alert! Watch out for your great enemy, the Devil. He prowls around like a roaring lion, looking for someone to devour. Stand firm against him and be strong in your faith. Remember that your family of believers all over the world is going through the same kind of suffering you are. In His kindness God called you to share in His eternal glory by means of Christ Jesus. So, after you have suffered a little while, he will restore,

support, and strengthen you, and he will place you on a firm foundation.

If your situation is not changing, you are not alone—He is with you, and you have the body of Christ to walk with you through it all. Above all, God promises to perfect all that concerns you, if not in the now, in the hereafter. It is undoubtedly written: **"Surely goodness and mercy shall follow me all the days of my life: and I will dwell in the house of the LORD forever"** (Psalm 23:6).

We also saw that creation and humanity have an archenemy—the perpetrator of evil—and that he is constantly inflicting pain, suffering, disaster, calamity, and death upon humanity. He is the source of all the evil we see in the world, and humans have also become His instrument by which he works through the iniquity that is in them.

We also saw that God sent Jesus Christ and the church, operating by the power of the Holy Spirit as the primary agent of good in the world. In addition, God set and established a system with delegated authority in the world as ministers of God and punishers of evil.

We saw that God mainly works all things for a purpose for which He made all things. The purpose which He accomplished in Christ was to make Jesus Christ the firstborn among many brethren. God is cultivating and plans to harvest sons from the earth. It was repeated constantly that God's power is for this purpose.

To make sense of the conflict that we often have when God seems not to use His power to help in times of trouble, pain, and suffering, we saw that God might not use His power to change a harmful situation if changing that situation will thwart His purpose of revealing and forming men to the image of His Son. He will demonstrate His infinite power speedily over a situation if it will help reveal His sons or bring the harvest of sons of God from among humanity. Furthermore, it became clear that God is powerful enough to change any painful situation that the Devil inflicts on humans outside of such purpose-driven reason. We set our hope on the promise of the everlasting God who is good to all.

However, some situations seem to defy all hope in this world. In such a case, we have the hope of the world to come. Paul knew this when he said, "If in Christ we have hope in this life only, we are of all people most to be pitied" (1 Corinthians 15:19).

It is to such a mysterious and inexplicable situation that defies all counsel, wisdom, prayer, anointing, etc., that the rest of this last chapter speaks considering God's eternal plan and purpose. Let us start from Deuteronomy 30:11, 15–16, 19:

> For this commandment which I command thee this day, it is not hidden from thee, neither is it far off…See, I have set before thee this day **life and good**, and **death and evil**. In that I command thee this day to love the LORD thy God, to walk in his ways, and to keep his commandments and his statutes and his judgments, that thou mayest live and multiply: and the LORD thy God shall bless thee in the land whither thou goest to possess it…I call heaven and earth to record this day against you, that I have set before you **life and death, blessing and cursing: therefore choose life**, that both thou and thy seed may live.

Deuteronomy 30:15 and 19 reveal that life and good are one while death and evil are also one. When good is effectuated, life is in expression, and death is in expression when evil is done. Little wonder that, in Genesis 2 and 3, the tree God placed in the garden is called the tree of the knowledge of good and evil. The good in that tree is tainted with evilness, which has contaminated it. This is the relative goodness that we see all over the world; it will always fail because it is based on selfishness. Therefore, it is not the goodness that produces eternal life as it is not the fruit of the Spirit and is below the standard of love, which is the expression of sonship (Matthew 5:45). Just as it was in the Garden of Eden

252

with Adam and Eve, God set life and death before the people of Israel.

The tree of the knowledge of good and evil is the tree that produces death as it contains evil. The tree of life is the tree that produces eternal life, and it has ultimate good in it. From Deuteronomy 30:15, we know that when it is good—it is life. Good and life are joined together with "and" in the text. No wonder when death is finally defeated, the only tree in the New Jerusalem in Revelation 22 is the tree of life. There, God has brought the restoration of all things. In Deuteronomy 30:19, God said, "Choose life." Such counsel reveals the character of God to us—His inherent goodness and His constant working to produce good (life) in every situation. He said to the people of Israel that they should choose life, although He has revealed to them that life and death exist; blessings and curses exist.

Revelation 21 and 22 are filled with the garden of Eden language and therefore describe a restoration by a new creation which includes and transcends that of Genesis when the Bible says things were good:

> Then I saw a new heaven and a new earth, for the first heaven and the first earth had passed away, and the sea was no more. And I saw the holy city, new Jerusalem, coming down out of heaven from God, prepared as a bride adorned for her husband. And I heard a loud voice from the throne saying, "Behold, the dwelling place of God is with man. He will dwell with them, and they will be his people, and God himself will be with them as their God. He will wipe away every tear from their eyes, and death shall be no more, neither shall there be mourning, nor crying, nor pain anymore, for the former things have passed away." And he who was seated on the throne said, **"Behold, I am making all things new." Also he said, "Write this down, for these words are trustworthy and true."** And he said to me, "It is done! I am the Alpha and the Omega, the beginning and the end. To the thirsty I will give from the spring of the water of life without

payment. **The one who conquers will have this heritage, and I will be his God and he will be my son.** But as for the cowardly, the faithless, the detestable, as for murderers, the sexually immoral, sorcerers, idolaters, and all liars, their portion will be in the lake that burns with fire and sulfur, which is the second death. (Revelation 21:1–8)

From verse 4, we see that God already has a master plan to deal with evil as He will make the former things go away. Whenever we buy things from stores, we often get a warranty that if it has a defect, it will be replaced with another. I believe that God created this current heaven and Earth with full warranty before the Devil stepped in to cause a defect. And that warranty comes with a guarantee that *God will make it all new*. God will replace this current state of things that pass away and create a new heaven and a new Earth where righteousness dwells, and there is no evil. Look around you—do you see anything broken, do you see anything in pain, sorrow, suffering, and dead? God says He is making it new because it is under warranty. Everything will be made new.

I think of my daughter and her "broken" body as I write this. To know that God is making all things new means that He is making my daughter's brain, eyes, legs, internal organs, hands, and every single part of her DNA and chromosomes new. In this, I rejoice in hope. I can only imagine what it will be like to see her perfectly whole in heaven, should we not see her complete restoration on the earth, for which I still believe God to accomplish supernaturally.

Who calls anything or action evil if it does not result in mourning, pain, disaster, and death? God will ultimately fill all things, and that is when He has already produced His overcomers, who are the sons he wanted to bring to glory (Revelation 21:7). Then He will wrap up the scripts and close the entire former things (which is the current creation—the present heaven and the earth that is under the power of the evil one) that are filled with evil and subject to bondage. When it is all said and done, all our lives will mean nothing. Only what we do in and for love as manifesting sonship will stand for eternity. What can you do today to love someone - an enemy, total stranger, or friend. Remember that love is why creation came into being, and love is the virtue that keeps and sustains creation. Love is the lifestyle of the Sons of God. (Matthew 5: 25, compare Romans 8:14 and Galatians 5:22).

You can find a sound biblical understanding of love in 1 Corinthians 13:1-13 (TPT):

> If I were to speak with eloquence in earth's many languages, and in the heavenly tongues of angels, yet I didn't express myself with love, my words would be reduced to the hollow sound of nothing more than a clanging cymbal. And if I were to have the gift of prophecy with a profound understanding of God's hidden secrets, and if I possessed unending supernatural knowledge, and if I had the greatest gift of faith that could move mountains, but have never learned to love, then I am nothing. And if I were to be so generous as to give away everything I owned to feed the poor, and to offer my body to be burned as a martyr, without the pure motive of love, I would gain nothing of value. Love is large and incredibly patient. Love is gentle and consistently kind to all. It refuses to be jealous when blessing comes to someone else. Love does not brag about one's achievements nor inflate its own importance. Love does not traffic in shame and disrespect, nor selfishly seek its own honor. Love is not easily irritated or quick to take offense. Love joyfully celebrates honesty and finds no delight in what is wrong. Love is a safe place of shelter, for it never stops believing the best for others. Love never takes failure as defeat, for it never gives up. Love never stops loving. It extends beyond the gift of prophecy, which eventually fades away. It is more enduring than tongues, which will one day fall silent. Love remains long after words of knowledge are forgotten. Our present knowledge and our prophecies are

but partial, but when love's perfection arrives, the partial will fade away. When I was a child, I spoke about childish matters, for I saw things like a child and reasoned like a child. But the day came when I matured, and I set aside my childish ways. For now, we see but a faint reflection of riddles and mysteries as though reflected in a mirror, but one day we will see face-to-face. My understanding is incomplete now, but one day I will understand everything, just as everything about me has been fully understood. **Until then, there are three things that remain: faith, hope, and love—yet love surpasses them all. So above all else, let love be the beautiful prize for which you run.**

Whatever you might be going through that seems inexplicable and defies all logical explanation within the bounds of your knowledge of God, let me say at this point to you that God is working, and He is making. He is working all things for good, which is primarily to conform you to the image of His Son, and He is making all things new. You might not see it, and you might not understand it. However, while you wait eagerly for the change to come, whether it will come in time as a foretaste of that which will be consummated in the fullness of time or it would manifest at the fullness of time, you must live for the praise of His glory as His sons in love. You must allow the life of His Son, Jesus Christ, to manifest in you. Sing praise to Him in His church and among those whom He called brethren. *To worship and live for the praise of His glory is one of the purposes of your existence, and as you do that, no matter the evil you experience in your life, the Son of God will manifest as either a miracle worker, the healer, the Savior, the Redeemer, or the fourth man ((the Son of God) in the fiery furnace.* And He will sit on the throne of your heart and declare to you,

Behold, I am making all things new. Also, He said, Write this down, for these words are trustworthy and true. (Revelation 21:5 ESV)

In the middle of the mystery, while it all seems unclear, this is the conclusion of the matter:

Ecclesiastes 12:13—"Fear God and obey His commandment—for this is the whole duty of man!"

Ecclesiastes 12:13 (AMPC)—**"All has been heard; the end of the matter is: Fear God [revere and worship Him, knowing that He is] and keep His commandments, for this is the whole of man [the full, original purpose of his creation, the object of God's providence, the root of character, the foundation of all happiness, the adjustment to all inharmonious circumstances and conditions under the sun] and the whole [duty] for every man."**

In all situations, whether good or bad in this present world, the highest response we can give is to fear and worship the Lord. And the highest form of worship is obedience and yielding of our body to God as a living sacrifice:

I appeal to you therefore, brothers, by the mercies of God, to **present your bodies as a living sacrifice,** holy and acceptable to God, **which is your spiritual worship"** (Romans 12:1).

As Job did while calamity befell him, rather than despair, he fell on His face and worshipped God. You know the end of the story for Job; God restored his fortune.

While the Devil throws calamity at you in this life, He intends to steal, kill, and destroy your heart and thereby produce death in this world and, in the world to come, the second death. Your response to the Devil is to put a fist in His face and say, "You could not sustain worshipping God in the beginning. You wanted Jesus to doubt His Father and worship you in the wilderness. You wanted Job to doubt God and worship you in the book of Job. You wanted Paul to doubt God and worship you in 2 Corinthians 12. Now you are coming for me as well. You wanted the three Hebrew men to doubt God and worship you when the Babylonian king cast them into the fairy furnace. You want me to doubt God and worship you so that I can spend my eternity in your hell. I say no to you, Satan. I say yes to God. I worship God. Even if He slays me, I will worship Him. I know that my God can save me from this fiery furnace; even if He does not, I will not bow. I will worship Him and no other god or demon or angels or you, Satan. All my worship, devotion, and obedience are to the Lord God Most High who rules in the affairs of men, and His royalty is expressed in eternal love even when I cannot see it. I know that my Redeemer lives, and He shall stand in the last days when he will make all things new." In this, I hope with my hope and anchor fixed on Jesus. This is true because **God is good, He does good, He is doing you good, and He is working everything together for your good within His good eternal purpose in this life and the one to come!**

Regardless of all the logic, rationale, inspiration, motivation, and explanation given in this book, I would like to submit to you that, beyond all explanation and attempt to make sense of evil, calamity, pain, and suffering, you must never forget that **God's dealings with us as His children are always surrounded with a silver line of mystery interwoven with His working. Trust Him and hope in Him, for you shall yet praise Him, if not in the world, certainly in the world to come.** For Jesus said, and he cannot lie, that "...It is finished!..."(John 19:30 KJV) and " ... "It is done! I am the Alpha and the Omega, the beginning and the end..." (Revelation 21:6). The principle of evil was finished at the cross of Jesus where He bore our pain, sorrow, oppression, grief, and the Iniquity of us all was laid on Him. (Isaiah 53:1-12). The driving force of evil is done at the end of time when God's eternal desire to have sons is accomplished for all eternity! (Revelation 21:6–7). It is finished and done for as many as have received Jesus in this world – the one who accomplished it all!!!!

God will tabernacle with humanity (Rev 21:3) and the desires of all the nations will be the Lord. (Haggai 2:6-7, Revelation 21:23–24)). At that time, there evil will be no more "...He will wipe away every tear from their eyes and eliminate death entirely. No one will mourn or weep any longer. The pain of wounds will no longer exist, for the old order has ceased..." (Revelation 21:4, TPT). There will only be life (Revelation 21:6; 22:1–2), goodness, bliss, peace, and joy forever and ever!!!! The reign of evil is gone forever. It is finished! It is done! Jesus Christ, the Son of God, did it all! Hallelujah!!!!

Shalom aleichem.

Be on the lookout for an upcoming book by the author. The book focuses on "The Paradox of our Faith." The title and details will be available on the author's website and social media platforms in the coming year.

Follow, listen to, and download the author's Dtransfer podcast on major podcasting platforms. Connect with a community of disciples and Jesus followers led by the author, Jesus Forever. Follow the Jesus Forever Page on Facebook and join the Disciples of Jesus Christ group.

Kindly consider leaving a review on Amazon for "Behold, I Make All Things New!"

Connect with Dr. Tunde Caleb Agboola:
drtundecalebagboola.com

The cover was designed by John Oyekola ("Mperor John").

Note: Ayanfeoluwa (meaning Beloved or Chosen of the Lord) is the correct spelling of our daughter's first name. ("Ayanfeoluna" is a misspelling of her name sent to the social security office from the hospital that has remained)

www.ingramcontent.com/pod-product-compliance
Lightning Source LLC
Chambersburg PA
CBHW020226130626
46549CB00005B/1757